THE HARVEST

by

Johnny L. Dudley

Inspirational Publishing Co. Inc.
Peterborough, NH 03458 U.S.A.

ISBN No. 0-930397-07-X
Inspirational Publishing Co. Inc.
PO Box 447
Peterborough, NH 03458 U.S.A.

The Harvest

Contents

1
The Two Mysteries

It was a hot, humid afternoon as I parked my pickup truck in the front yard of a slightly tilted frame house on the outskirts of town. Dogs of all shapes and sizes seemed to materialize, greeting me with a diversity of wags and barks, as I made my way to the rear of the house. Behind the house, long rows of greenhouses emerged out of an immense growth of ugly dog fennel weeds. A well-worn path led me through the ugly plants to the front door of the first plastic house.

Pushing my way through the door, I stepped into a controlled environment where all of the necessary ingredients for the germination of a seed were carefully regulated. Long rows of tables sagged with the weight of hundreds of vessels of potting soil that were neatly arranged under a complex network of irrigation pipes. Workers carefully tended their needs, and each vessel brought forth fruit according to the seed which the husbandman of the greenhouse had sown.

And so it is with the universe. God has created an environment that houses a world full of "clay vessels"...people (2 Cor. 4:7). Each vessel is a fertile container endowed with the capacity to germinate the seed of truth, which is referred to in Scripture as the "wheat." Unfortunately, we are not restricted to the seed of the wheat only but are also able to receive and germinate the engraftable seed of deception...the tare.

The wheat is the good seed of the Word of God sown by the Son of man (Matt. 13:37). Those who receive and nurture the good seed are the children of the kingdom (Matt. 13:38). *The wheat is the seed of truth (God's Word), that matures into the fruit of understanding, which causes us to humble ourselves before God.*

The tare is the seed that is sown by the devil (Matt. 13:39). Those who receive and nurture the seed of the tare are the children of the devil (Matt. 13:38). *The tare is a seed of deception, that matures into the fruit of confusion, so that we act with arrogance before God.*

The tare is indistinguishable from wheat while the two are growing into blade. But when they become ear, they can be separated without difficulty, for it is by their fruits that they are known (Matt. 7:15–20).

And so it is with the world. Two seeds are sown in the earth. Both are bringing forth a mystery. The seed of the wheat is bringing forth the "Mystery of God...he hath declared to his servants the prophets" (Rev. 10:7). The seed of the tare is bringing forth "The mystery of iniquity" (2 Thess. 2:7). Both seeds will continue to grow together until the end of the age and the time of the harvest (Matt. 13:30).

There is enmity between them! (Gen. 3:15).

The Mystery of God

The seed of the Word of God has been sown in the earth to bring forth a harvest (James 5:7). That God was after a harvest was a mystery to the Hebrew prophets (Rom. 16:25–26) and is often misunderstood by the New Testament church.

Men have taught the concept that God has engineered redemption in order that He might restore man to the unfallen state of Adam. However, Adam was never the completed product. He did not fully reflect the image of God.

In the Genesis account of creation, it is recorded that God said, "Let us make man in our image, after our likeness" (Gen. 1:26). He then began the creation process by forming Adam from the dust of the earth. But Adam was not finished, he did not bear the perfect image of his creator.

There are two key areas in Adam's nature which fall drastically short of reflecting God's image. These character flaws openly demonstrate that God has not yet completed His creation process in Adam. Adam was: (1) unable to resist sin and walk in perfect obedience, and (2) not able to walk in love. When Adam was confronted with his sin, he immediately demonstrates his character flaws by shifting the blame to Eve. He was unwilling to lay down his life for her.

God is omniscient. Therefore, His infinite understanding enables Him to speak of things that are not as though they were (Rom. 4:17; Ps. 147:5). He is able to declare the end from the beginning, and from ancient times He declares the things that are not yet done (Isa. 46:10). Therefore, due to His ability to speak of the future as though it were the present, He was able to declare that man was made in His image. This declaration was based entirely upon the immutability of His word, but not upon what had already transpired.

God's statement that man was created in His image was not a joyful conclusion of His work. Rather, it was the first universal proclamation of His objective. His objective is to bring forth many reproductions of Christ (Rom. 8:29).

Christ is the first man made totally in the image of the Father! He is perfect in obedience and love, and redeemed man is now being made into the image of Christ.

Christ is the prototype, the original model that we are being patterned after. Man is the earthen culture (that is, prepared nutrient). We are vessels made from dust (Gen. 2:7; 3:19; Ecc. 3:20) with the capacity to incubate and germinate the Word of God. The Word of God is "engrafted" into the human heart to reproduce after its kind (James 1:21). We are presently in the process of being made into the image of the original prototype—Jesus Christ, who is the Word of God (John 1:14).

The Genesis account of creation teaches us that God spoke the worlds into existence but formed man from dust. However, dust cannot reflect the image of God. God is, therefore, creating man by speaking him into existence just like He did the worlds. He is sending forth His Word—as the dew from heaven—to bud in the heart of His clay vessels, man. His Word will not return void but shall accomplish that which He pleases (Isa. 55:11).

God's Word reflects His image: Dust could never fulfill that expression. His Word is bringing forth a harvest of men created in His image. We will one day shed these containers of corruptible dust to allow the incorruptible seed of His Word, which has been germinating inside of us, to be raised in His likeness. The Word of God (Jesus) was resurrected on that first Easter morning. And it is the Word of God, which has been sown in us, that will be resurrected at the last trump. Made in His likeness, we will then live and reign with Him forever (1 Peter 1:23).

God the Father is like a husbandman who is patiently waiting for the earth to bring forth a harvest (James 5:7). He first made a seed into His perfect image: that seed is Christ (Gal. 3:16). Jesus then made the universe (John 1:3). The universe has unlimited boundaries that house countless principalities and dominions (Col. 1:16). Finally, this world was brought forth in the midst of the universe as a field (Matt. 13:38), for the sowing and reproducing of the righteous seed—Jesus.

Although man is the last of all creation, he is being brought forth as the highest in authority of all of the created beings—fulfilling the law that the last shall be first.

Redeemed man will be first in rank of all of the created beings of the universe. He will reign with Christ as the third in power over all of creation. The first in authority is the person of God the Father; the second is the Word of God, Christ; and the third will be the bride of Christ, the Church. Our authority will be of the Father because He will inhabit us by His Holy Spirit (Eph. 2:22).

While God is in the process of making man in His image, we are being observed by a great cloud of witnesses (Heb. 12:1). These witnesses are, in part, the principalities and powers that Christ has previously created in heavenly places. Throughout the process of creating man into the image of God, these principalities and dominions of creation past are learning of God's manifold wisdom (Eph. 3:10).

Through the observation of the earth, God is teaching these heavenly dominions the drastic wages of sin. They are also learning of His grace, mercy, endless love, and His severity.

The long process of man's redemption is *not* a product of clever engineering designed after the fall of Adam. *God knew man was going to fall before the worlds were framed* (1 Cor. 2:7; Eph. 1:4; 2 Tim. 1:9; 1 Peter 1:18-20; Rev. 13:8). Man's fall was predetermined in the heart of God. It is a necessary step in the creative process of making man in His image.

Because of man's destiny, it is necessary that he should first experience the devastating effects of being separated from God through the sin of pride. Man's destiny is perfection in Christ. We are to walk in an intimate fellowship with the Most High God, reigning with His son as priests and kings throughout all of the created universe (Rev. 1:6). This position will make us extremely vulnerable to the sin of pride. Therefore, God is preparing us by allowing us to have an experiential knowledge of the fruit of pride before we are awarded our inheritance. Having lived in darkness, we will never again be enticed by pride once we are brought into His light.

Unlike Lucifer, we will bear the beauty of perfection in humility. We will never again assume that our strength and glory is of ourselves. We will eternally express the praise of the glory of His marvelous grace, rejoicing in Him forever (Eph. 1:6).

The part of God's plan that required man to fall (in order to bring him to glory), is made even more perfect by the inclusion of Christ. Christ is the captain of our faith. As the captain, He also was required to have an experiential knowledge of the effects of sin. At Calvary, Christ experienced the horror of being separated from the Father by the sins of man. It was appropriate that He was made perfect through suffering in order that He would be sensitive to our weaknesses in every way (Heb. 2:10).

Although Christ has tasted the bitterness of sin, His response to it was different than ours. He endured sin for us, but man has embraced sin as a first love.

Through Calvary, Christ has provided a way for man to escape the wages of sin. He has ransomed us from death and is now sowing His eternal nature into the core of our being. He is life, and life is being engrafted into us. He is transforming us to His nature and inhabiting us with His spirit. He is building us together into a holy habitation of God through the Spirit, a holy tabernacle (1 Cor. 3:9, 16; 1 Cor. 6:19; Eph. 2:22).

The tabernacle He is building for the Spirit of God is not a physical building, as we would picture in our mind. It is a nation of redeemed men constructed into the image of Christ. We are being prepared to house the Spirit of the living God so that He might express himself through us throughout all of the created universe. Christ is using the intense heat and pressure of our environment to bring us into total devotion to the Father, so that we will be fitting vessels to fulfill the purpose of our calling.

We are becoming stones of unwavering love toward the Father—living stones harvested from all nations. These stones are human cultures of dust who are being transformed into the eternal nature of God by engrafting the seed of His Word into their hearts.

Jesus is gathering these stones out of all nations and engrafting them into himself, the vine of Israel, as you would engraft wild olive branches into a cultured olive tree. Each of these stones will be able to express the nature of God's Spirit in a special way. All of us together comprise the Temple that Christ is building. We are being built upon the foundation that was laid by the revelations of the apostles and prophets. Jesus is both the master architect and the chief cornerstone of the Temple. In Him, all the building is being fitly framed together and is growing into a holy temple in the Lord. Once completed, the Spirit of God will dwell in us (His Temple) without measure.

Like a many-faceted diamond that defines, reveals, and expresses the seven different colors of the light which flows through it, we are being built into a many-faceted Temple that will externally express the complex nature of the seven spirits of God (see Rev. 1:4; 3:1; 4:5; 5:6). Each of us are patterned after Christ; yet, each of us expresses a unique facet of the nature of God.

The true purpose of God for man was a mystery to the Hebrew prophets. They spoke of it and prophesied about it, but they were not able to fully understand the magnitude of what God is doing (Eph. 3:5; Col. 1:26).

God has used the Hebrew nation and its prophets to paint a portrait. Little by little, He created a verbal portrait of His nature and His purpose to the world through a prophetic scenario. Each of the Old Testament characters play a part in the portrait of God.

When the portrait was complete and the timing was right, He then revealed the fullness of His verbal portrait in the flesh of one man. . . Jesus. Jesus is the portrait.

The world could not comprehend the fullness of what God had done for us in Christ. Therefore, He raised up apostles to assimilate the Scriptures and to fully express Christ through the power of the Holy Spirit. The apostles were used by God to remove the veil that had covered the prophetic portrait—thus revealing a full revelation of Christ. This revelation of Christ is the foundation rock upon which He is building His Church (Matt. 16:18).

Christ is the full expression of the Word of God. He is the portrait of the Father that was unveiled at calvary for all to see. He is the firstborn of many brethren who are being made into His likeness. He is the firstfruit of the harvest of the earth, and as a firstfruit, He was made a Holy sacrifice unto Jehovah for the purification of His brethren. We are the harvest of the earth. Therefore, through the sacrificial giving of Christ, both He that sanctifieth and they who are sanctified are all of one. The Bible says, "For which cause He is not ashamed to call them brethren" (Heb. 2:11) and "For if the firstfruit be holy, the lump is also holy and if the root be holy, so are the branches" (Rom. 11:16).

The mystery of God, which was hidden in the prophetic portrait, is that Christ (the seed of God, according to Gal. 3:16) is sown within us, a precious seed. Through the process of engrafting himself into us, He is bringing forth a harvest of men transformed into the glory of His likeness from the inside out (2 Cor. 3:18).

God spoke of this phenomenal calling from the very beginning. The first promise of the seed which was to bring forth this mysterious harvest was given to Eve, the mother of all living (Gen. 3:15, 20). The nature of the seed was then carried through her offspring from Seth to Noah, carefully preserved through the flood in Shem (Noah's son), and expressed to us bit by bit through the nation of Israel.

The seed of God's Word was incubated for centuries in the nation of Israel like the seed of a fruit which incubates in its own flesh. Then, at the appointed time the seed of the Word of God was revealed in its entirety in the flesh of one man—Jesus. Out of the spiritual dryness of Israel He came forth as the full revelation of the seed of God's Word. He walked among us, allowing us to behold the glory of God in Him and to handle Him with our hands (1 John 1).

Being a people who dwell in darkness, we could not comprehend the light of the world—Jesus. His light intimidated us and provoked us to jealousy, so we crucified Him and sowed Him in the earth. After three days, He came forth a vine, as a root out of the spiritually dry ground of Israel (Isa. 53; Rom. 15:12).

The vine (Jesus) then ascended to the right hand of

the Father and began to build the Temple of God by engrafting the branches (men from all nations) into himself (Zech. 6:12; Rom. 11:17; John 15:1).

The church that Christ is building was a mystery to the prophets, but is the true objective of God. Christ is the promised seed, and He is being engrafted into those that are thirsty, bringing forth His likeness in each of us. Therefore, we have confidence that we will partake of his glory (Col. 1:27).

In Scripture, the wheat, the Word of God, the promised seed, and Jesus are synonymous terms. The wheat is being sown in the hearts of men. One of its greatest functions is to bring forth the humility of Christ in each of us. *True humility comes when we begin to understand the glory of God in relation to the degenerate conditon of the human heart.* The highest form of humility is demonstrated by unconditional trust in God. That kind of trust requires a total reconstruction of the whole man by God's Word.

If we nurture God's Word in our hearts, it will bring forth humility, purity, meekness, and the privilege of enjoying the promised inheritance of Abraham.

Abraham was promised the abiding presence of the person of God as his exceeding great reward (Gen. 15:1). Jesus has that abiding presence without measure (John 3:34). We are being made into the image of Jesus. Therefore, those who yield to construction by the Word of Truth will also bear His glory. We are the heirs of the promise which was made to Abraham and demonstrated in Christ. Like Jesus, *we will bear the glorious spirit of God without measure. He is our exceeding great reward.*

We are the fruit of the Word of God—the Church. The Church is the "Mystery of God" that was declared to the prophets of old. Our King is Jesus. He is the seed and the firstfruit of the Word of God, and "in the days. . . when he [THE SEVENTH ANGEL] shall begin to sound his trumpet, the mystery of God should be finished, as he hath declared to his servants the prophets." (Rev. 10:7).

The Mystery of Iniquity
Due to the ability of the Father to know the future, He knew even before He created him that Lucifer (Satan) was going to fall. Satan's fall stimulates one of the greatest questions of all times. "Why did God create Satan?"

To answer that, it is necessary to reiterate the objective of God in His creation of man. God is creating a nation of just men made perfect (Heb. 12:23). Each of us are to house the Spirit of God without measure as perfect expressions of Him. Our destiny is to reign with Christ as priests and kings throughout all of the created universe. We are, therefore, being made perfect through the trying of our faith (James 1:2-4).

Perfection is a dangerous commodity, as is demonstrated in the fall of Satan. Satan was created perfect, but he was corrupted when his mind began to dwell on his own brightness. Eventually, the vain imaginations of his heart became such a reality to him that he believed he could usurp the throne of his Creator and be like the most high. The seed of deception had matured in his heart, bringing forth the fruit of confusion. He was, thereby, defiled in the innermost

12

sanctuaries of his heart, and began to walk with arrogance before his Creator (Ezek. 28:1–19; Isa. 14:13, 14).

The glory that God had bestowed on Satan proved to be very difficult to handle. Ezekiel records that the multitude of his successes laid the groundwork for the flatteries that defiled his heart (Ezek. 28:16, 18). Had he known *experientially* the effects of sin, he would never have entertained the thoughts of exalting himself above God.

Satan's fate would also befall the sons of man, if God were simply to create us and place us into our positions of universal authority. Therefore, God in His infinite wisdom instituted a plan. His plan is to teach us experientially the wages of sin before He exalts us to our inheritance. We are being brought through darkness into His light. Having lived in darkness, we will adhere to the light with absolute devotion.

Our hearts are being transformed. We are not learning to overcome sin by discipline, which has a show of will worship and personal pride. Jesus is recreating our innermost heart, aligning it with His heart in a hatred for sin and a love for righteousness (Ps. 45:7). This change of the heart is superior to discipline in that the lure of sin will no longer entice us. Had the Father created us perfect in beauty and wisdom first, as He did Satan, we would always have the same vulnerability to pride that wrought the destruction of Satan and the fall of Adam. There would always be the lingering desire to taste and see for ourselves.

Satan is a necessary instrument in the bringing forth of the many sons of God—the Church. He is the source of trials and tribulations, which are necessary to prepare us to reign in the universe. We are being brought forth through much tribulation (Acts 14:22). Satan is, therefore, as much a part of God's plan to bring forth the sons of God as is Judas or Pharoah (Rom. 9:17-23).

Satan is being used by God to teach us, as well as the rest of creation, the folly of pride. It is through his rebellion that we are learning about the devastating recourse of sin. Therefore, once we have come into our inheritance, we will never again be enticed by sin.

The parable of the wheat and the tare teaches us that Satan has sowed his seed into the heart of man. The seed he sowed is deception, and it has brought forth a confusion in man that Paul has labeled the "mystery of iniquity" (2 Thess. 2:7).

The book of Genesis records the first implanting of Satan's seed as he subtly labored to sow the tare into the heart of Eve. To entice here, *he focused her attention on herself and what she could be.* Masterfully, he then planted seeds of doubt, until her mind began to question the integrity of God's Word. She became unstable; her imagination began to delight in the proud fantasies of the serpent's deception. The thought of being as God consumed her mind, so that the fruit of her imagination became enticingly pleasant to her eyes.

The tare had been sown. Satan had enticed Eve into violating one of the principles of the first commandment, which is to love God with all of your mind, bringing every thought into captivity and aligning it with God's Word. The seed of deception began to germinate in the heart of Eve, bringing forth a fire in the midst

of her innermost sanctuary (Ezek. 28:18). She began
to duplicate the desire of Satan in her heart, saying. . . "I will be like the Most High!" (See Gen. 3:5,
where Satan told Eve, "ye shall be as gods"). It was
just a matter of time before the seed in her heart
manifested itself as an outward work of transgression
against the laws of God.

She then ate of the forbidden tree, and like Satan,
she sought to involve someone else in her sin—Adam.
And the seed continued to grow.

The seed was carried through the flood by Ham and
demonstrated to the world through the nations that he
fathered.[1] To state that all of the descendants of Ham
are wicked would be as incorrect as stating that all of
the descendants of Shem are righteous. The point I wish
to make, however, is that through the descendants of
these two men, God has taught us the nature of the
two seeds. The Lord has used the descendants of Ham
to teach the nature and fruit of the tare, as he has also
used the descendants of Shem (Israel), to teach the
nature and fruit of the wheat.

The first clear portrait of the fruit of the tare
blossomed through Nimrod, the grandson of Ham.
Nimrod established Babel, the city of confusion (Babel
means confusion). Out of the heart of the people of
Babel, we again see the mature spirit of pride as they
set their heart to make a name for themselves (Gen.
11:4). They desired to be independent of God, to be
their own strength. Their desire was self-exaltation, and
they trusted in their own capabilities.

Self-exaltation is the core of pride, and pride is the
root of sin. It emanates an arrogant spirit and offends

the meek in heart. *Pride is confusion. It has no comprehension of the glory of God in relation to the degenerate condition of the human heart.*

The highest form of pride is demonstrated in unrepentent religious leaders who strive to achieve righteousness through works. They strive to have the appearance of righteousness, but in reality they are blind leaders of the blind.

When Jesus addressed the religious leaders of the nation of Israel, He exposed the mature fruit of the tare. He called them white-washed sepulchres who, on the inside, were full of dead men's bones (Matt. 23:27). In other words, outwardly they were imitators of holiness, proud of their works. But they were unable to recognize the arrogance of their hearts. The father of the seed that they bore was the devil, yet they assumed a relationship with God based on their own righteous acts.

Jesus did not reject people bound in sin; He had compassion on them and provided a means of deliverance by the shedding of His blood. However, He resisted those who arrogantly exalted themselves as having superior achievements of righteousness. There is no greater demonstration of pride and arrogance than to claim equality with God or acceptance by Him because of one's own works!

The seed of the tare has been reproducing and maturing in the earth since the fall of Adam. It has grown into a consuming vine that has engulfed the hearts of men, convincing them that they are inherently good, having no need of a Savior. The fruit of that vine will be harvested and burned at the end of the age (Matt. 13:38–42).

The Lord speaks of the mysterious vine of iniquity in the feminine gender, calling it a whore. In Rev. 17:5, he gives the mature vine of iniquity an appropriate title.

MYSTERY BABYLON THE GREAT
[the great mystery of confusion],
THE MOTHER OF HARLOTS
[matron prostitute of religion, AND
ABOMINATIONS OF THE EARTH
[vile before God, defiling man].

There are many branches of man-made religious systems with the outward appearance of chastity. They teach purity, love, and all of the good attributes of the Spirit of God. They have the external appearance of righteousness through discipline, but their spirit exposes the unregenerated condition of their heart. The inner motivations of these men have *not* been remade by the Word of God, and secretly, they commit fornication with the earth for gain. They have the outward appearance of righteousness but they are the prostitutes of religion. The inhabitants of the earth have been made drunk with the wine of their deception (Rev. 17:2).

Throughout history, it has been these apostate religious systems that have slain the righteous while they strove for power and self-gratification. Political persecutions have been few in relation to the persecutions wrought through religious leaders. It was one of these systems of arrogant religious hypocrosy which jealously engineered the crucifixion of the prince of life (Acts 3:15).

Like the wheat, the tare is the bride of her lord. He

is the lord of the mystery of iniquity and he is yet to be revealed in the flesh—imitating Jesus. He will appear to be of God, but he will be the epitome of arrogance—the antichrist. As Christ is the seed of the wheat made flesh, the antichrist will be the seed of the tare made flesh. The world will be deceived by him and will pursue him in a fervent heat.

In summary, the seed of deception that was first sown in the garden of Eden has brought forth a mystery of iniquity, confusing men. It manifested itself in Babel after the flood and is continuing to grow into maturity in the earth. It has all of the appearance and conversation of religion, but it emanates the spirit of pride instead of humility. Like the mystery of God, it is growing into maturity.

At the end of this age, both mysteries will be mature in the earth; ripe for harvest. It is the conflict of these two mysteries, when they grow into maturity, that will bring forth the *great tribulation*.

2
A Knowledge of the Times

The two mysteries, which have sprouted from the seeds of the wheat and the tare, are approaching maturity in the earth. This is evident because Israel has become a nation again after two thousand years of dispersion, revealing that the spring of the age is upon us and the time of the fruit is near. There is also a gentle stirring in the hearts of the saints, an inner awareness that the climax of the age is rapidly approaching.

The questions that now arise within us are:

(1) When will the wheat (mystery of God) be harvested (raptured) into God's presence?

(2) When will the tare (mystery Babylon) be harvested for judgment?

(3) When will the Lord return and reign as the prince of peace?

These questions are the center of attention when discussing biblical prophecy. Yet they remain unsettled in the hearts of most believers. The reason satisfaction has eluded us is that we have failed to properly label and understand the underlying question that really disturbs us. It is a question that continues to cast a shadow of doubt over everything we learn. That question is:

> (4) Does God really desire His people to know the answers to the first three questions (above), or is the two-fold harvest of the wheat and tare (the two mysteries), and the day of His coming in power and glory (the day of the Lord) to remain a secret until it transpires, surprising even the Church?

This chapter is devoted to clarifying the answer to the latter question (4). That answer is: Yes! God *does* desire His people to know the times and seasons, so that they will not be caught by surprise.

> But ye, brethern, are not in darkness, that that day should overtake you as a thief. (1 Thess. 5:4)

> Surely the Lord God will do nothing, but he revealeth his secret unto his servants the prophets. (Amos 3:7)

In order to develop a sound foundation for the solution to question (4), let us first examine major biblical events that have already transpired. In each of these past events, God has consistently informed His people in advance as to *what* was going to happen and *when* it was to take place. The keys of understanding in each of these events were not exposed for the whole world to see, but were revealed only to those who loved the Lord God with all of their heart. *God has always informed the people who walk with Him in advance as to His intentions.*

The Flood

The flood did not come as a surprise to the people who walked with God in the earth; however, the only one recorded as walking with God was Noah. Noah was a just man, and perfect in his generation. Therefore, God told Noah what He was going to do in advance.

God said to Noah, "The end of all flesh is come before me; for the earth is filled with violence through them; and, behold, I will destroy them with the earth" (Gen. 6:13).

God not only told Noah the destiny of the wicked, but He also completely explained how He was going to preserve Noah and his seed (Gen. 6:18).

God did not dump this revelation on Noah and leave him wondering when all of it was going to happen. He took the time to explain to Noah what had to be done in order to prepare.

He did not wait until the last minute so that Noah would have to strive to build the ark in time. God gave Noah sufficient notice so that, through a consistent application of the knowledge God had imparted, Noah was able to fulfill his ministry.

When Noah was prepared, God informed him that

he had seven days to load the ark with his family and cargo. Noah faithfully obeyed all that the Lord required of him. Therefore, God faithfully preserved him through the judgment.

God was faithful to tell Noah *what* He was going to do and *when* He was going to do it!

The Exodus

The sojourn of Abraham's seed in Egypt was no surprise. Before Issac was born, God told Abraham that his seed would be a stranger in a land that was not theirs. He told Abraham that they would serve the people of that land under affliction for four-hundred years, and that He would afterwards judge the people who had afflicted them. He also told Abraham that He would bring his descendents out of that land with great substance, and use them to judge the Amorites (the original inhabitants of the land of Canaan whose iniquity would be full, ready for judgment) (Gen. 15:13–16).

Four centuries had lapsed when Moses appeared on the scene. God was right on time. It is amazing that the people did not readily receive Moses, because God had told them ahead of time that He would bring them out of bondage after four-hundred years. They should have known that Moses was going to lead them, simply by the timing of his appearance. They resisted Moses, just like they resisted Christ, because they were not aware of the time of their visitation.

The point that I wish to make, however, is that God told His people in advance *what* He was going to do and *when* He was going to do it. *The responsibility to remain aware of the times rested on the people.*

The Babylonian Captivity

Moses had been used by God to carefully define the lifestyle the Jews needed to develop in order to receive His blessings. The Jews consistently violated every principle of life that God had set before them, including the sabbatical year.[1]

Because they would not obey the words of the Lord, He raised up the prophet Jeremiah to warn them of coming judgment. The Word of the Lord that came through Jeremiah told the Jews that God was going to give them into the hands of the king of Babylon. They were going to experience total devastation, and they would be an astonishment and a byword to the surrounding nations. The voice of mirth and the voice of gladness would be taken from them, and the whole land would be a desolation and an astonishment; and they would serve the king of Babylon for seventy years.

After seventy years of captivity were ended, God was going to bring them back and punish the king of Babylon (Jer. 25:8–12).

God told the Jews what He was going to do, and when it was going to take place. He told them how long it was going to last and when it would be over. The Jews chose not to listen.

The Messiah

The seventy years of Babylonian captivity were almost fulfilled when the prophet Daniel appealed to God for knowledge of what the future held for the nation of Israel. God honored Daniel and his appeal, and opened to Daniel an understanding of the future in a vision that someone has properly labeled "history's greatest prophecy" (see Dan. 9).

In Daniel's vision of the seventy weeks, he understood that there would be a time span of sixty-nine weeks of years (483), which would *begin with the decree to restore Jerusalem* and *climax with the coming of the Messiah to be cut off, or slain for the people* (Dan. 9:25–26). In other words, Daniel was told in advance what the event would be that would trigger the 483-year countdown to the coming of the Messiah.

Jesus entered Jerusalem on the exact day appointed—exactly 483 years after Artaxerxes (King of Persia) issued the decree to restore and rebuild Jerusalem (Neh. 2:5–6). Upon his entry, the religious leaders of the day rebuked him for allowing His disciples to quote the Messianic Psalm: That Psalm was to be proclaimed only when the Messiah entered Jerusalem.

Jesus responded, "I tell you that, if these should hold their peace, the stones would immediately cry out" (Luke 19:38–40).

Jesus was right on time, in accordance with the words of the prophets. In order for the Jews to have known beyond a shadow of a doubt that Jesus was the Messiah, they needed only to have been aware of what time it was.

When Jesus beheld the city of Jerusalem, He wept over it and began to speak of the judgment that was to come. Jerusalem was going to be judged *because they knew not the time of their visitation* (Luke 19:41–44).

Jesus could not have allowed judgment to come upon Jerusalem for their lack of knowledge of the time if He had not first provided a complete and clear prophetic scenario of exactly when He was to come.

Herein lies a very important and vital point that must

be understood *before* we will ever grasp the fullness of scriptural teaching. The point is that *God has never left His people in the dark as to the time of fulfillment of any major event.* He was explicit in His timing with Noah concerning the flood. He gave Abraham understanding as to the length of time his seed was to be in Egypt. He forewarned Israel through Jeremiah of the Babylonian captivity and how long it would last. And He gave the prophet Daniel a complete outline of history before it happened, including a clear picture as to the exact day when the Messiah was to enter Jerusalem.

Does the Lord desire His beloved to be aware of the time of His second coming as well? Absolutely.

Jesus gave us points of reference concerning His second coming and the harvesting of the wheat and the tares, just like He did concerning His first coming. These are reference points which are yet future to us, like the decree to reconstruct Jerusalem was an event still in the future to Daniel.

The Lord has given us these points of reference so that we can discern the times and seasons. The reference points are given so that the last generation of the true bride will not be caught by surprise. He has warned us not to be caught as though a thief had entered our house but to watch and observe the times. We are not to be in darkness so that the day of the Lord should overtake us as a thief (1 Thess. 5:4, 5).

According to Paul, the only people who will be unaware of the times are those destined for destruction (1 Thess. 5:3). It will be like the days of Noah and Lot. On those days, the only people who were surprised were the ones who were to be judged (Luke 17:26–30).

Israel was told in advance the exact time that the Messiah would enter Jerusalem. It was because of their failure to properly watch for His coming that they were judged. Like Israel, we have a responsibility to understand the timepieces which the Lord has given us. We do not have to be caught by surprise. We should be able to discern the fulfillment of prophetic events and not be discouraged by the onslaught of sin. The coming days of calamity will cause those who love the Lord and are aware of His promises to lift their heads and look for His redemption (Luke 21:28).[2]

3
The Timepieces

God is our Father. As a father, He lovingly provides the necessities of life for us. One of the greatest necessities in life is a vision of our destiny; for where there is no vision, the people perish (Prov. 29:18). To implant vision, God has always informed His people as to His intentions in the earth, as would a husband to a wife or a father to a son.

Even in the judgment of Sodom, He was not willing to act without first notifying Abraham. In the heart of God was a burning desire to share with Abraham all of His intentions toward the earth (Gen. 18:17). The desire to relate His heart to us, Abraham's descendents through faith, continues to be a part of His character, even in these last days.

God has always informed His people as to the timing of major events. He has also held us responsible to listen and respond. Therefore, we should diligently seek to understand the key events that unlock the time of the return of our Lord and the harvest of the two mysteries—the wheat and the tare.

There are timepieces recorded in Scripture which will

provide those who are diligently watching with a knowledge of the times. Two of these timepieces are clearly defined in 2 Thess. 2:1–3:

> Now we beseech you, brethren, by *the coming of our Lord Jesus Christ*, and by our *gathering together unto him*. That ye be not soon shaken in mind, or be troubled, neither by spirit, nor by word, nor by letter as from us, as that the day of Christ is at hand. Let no man deceive you by any means: *For that day shall not come, except there come a falling away first, and that man of sin be revealed, the son of perdition* [antichrist]. (Italics mine)

Paul states in this passage that we should let no man deceive us. The coming of the Lord and our gathering together unto Him [the rapture] will not transpire until two things happen first: (1) A great falling away, and (2) that the man of sin be revealed.

Our hope is in the Lord's coming, but history's time clock is triggered by these two events.

As Israel was given the signs of the time when the first coming of the Messiah would occur, we the church are given the signs of the time as to when the Lord will gather the fruit of His seed (wheat) and will return in power and glory.

As Daniel's attention would have been drawn to looking for the decree to restore Jerusalem, we should be looking toward the great falling away of professing believers and the revealing of the man of sin, the antichrist.

Jesus placed these two events in their proper sequence in the twenty-fourth chapter of Matthew. His disciples asked the question: "What shall be the sign of thy coming, and of the end of the world?" (Matt. 24:3).

Two of the signs that Jesus gave in response to their question were the *great falling away* (Matt. 24:12–13) and the *revealing of the man of sin* (Matt. 24:15).

Matthew 24 is a synopsis of the events that will usher in the climax of the age. Jesus first discussed a period of time which He defined as the "beginning of sorrows" (vs. 8). Like birthpains, unstable world conditions will crescendo into the climax of this age, when there will be a universal persecution of the beloved (verse 9). As the price of obedience to Christ increases, many shall be offended, hating and betraying those whom they once called brethren (v. 10). Many false prophets will arise among the believers and seek to draw them away (v. 11). The world will continually increase in immorality, and many of those who once bore a love for the Lord Jesus Christ will become cold and indifferent. They will unite themselves with those "gods"— the lust of the eye and the pride of life (hence, a great falling away—vv. 12, 13). Through it all, there will remain a people who cannot be bought. They will continue to proclaim the gospel of the Lord Jesus to all nations (vv. 13, 14). As the chaos of uncertainty and immorality peaks, then the end shall come, and the abomination of desolation (the antichrist) shall reveal himself in the holy place (vv. 14, 15). Then those who are in Judea will flee for their lives (vv. 16–20). And, after the revealing of the antichrist in the holy place, there shall be great tribulation, such as has not been from the beginning of the world until this time (v. 21).

Immediately after the tributional period, the Lord will return, and the elect will be gathered (vv. 29–31).

The disciples asked Jesus, "What shall be the sign of thy coming?" His reply was that *after* the great falling away, and *after* the revelation of the antichrist, there would be a time of great tribulation. And, after the great tribulation, He will then come and gather His elect.

The *method* of gathering the elect, in this passage, clearly defines the elect as being the Church. The Church is the only people who will be gathered from the four winds of heaven (harvested)—*not Israel.* Israel will not be harvested in the same manner as the Church, but will remain in the earth until the literal return of the Lord and His saints, upon the mount of Olives (Zech. 14:3–11).

Jesus stated that world conditions are going to get progressively worse until, at last, many will fall away from their love for the Lord. The antichrist will then be revealed in the temple. *His desecration of the temple will be the event that begins the great tribulation* (Matt. 24:15–21). Remember, Paul stated that these two things must happen before the Lord Jesus comes and we are gathered together unto Him (2 Thess. 2:1–3).

Jesus did not foretell these events so that the unbelievers would have some interesting reading to occupy their time during the tribulation. Rather, this passage, as well as the whole Bible, is written for the benefit of his people, so that by recognizing the signs of the times we might have a *vision* of our destinies and *persevere* through the hardships ahead (Matt.

24:13). Only those who are abiding in Christ, drawing strength from His love, and are content to abide under His lordship will be able to stand in the coming days of calamity. For false Christs and false prophets shall begin to deceive the whole world with great signs and wonders, so that, if it were possible, they would even deceive the elect (the Church).

The 'elect' are not those born after the flesh of Abraham (Israel), but rather those who are the children of the promise (Church) that are drawn out of all nations (Rom. 9:6–11; Col. 3:11–12). If the elect will be here to see the antichrist and his prophet, there is no way that the Chruch could have already been removed (raptured) from the earth. Jesus has told us beforehand, so that we will not be deceived and fall (Matt. 24:25).

Second Thessalonians 2:7 tells us that the revealing of the antichrist is presently being restrained. Many have believed that the restraining force which Paul speaks of is the Holy Spirit, resident in the church, and that the Church must be removed out of the earth (raptured) for the antichrist to be revealed.

Although the Holy Spirit is the restraining force, and He does reside in the Church, there is nothing in that verse that implies in any way that He or the Church is removed out of the earth. The Spirit of God is omnipresent (Ps. 139:7–8). To state that He is removed from the earth is a statement that is contrary to His nature and is an assumption that has absolutely no foundation. Verse seven merely states that the restraining force will quite restraining—that is, it will be taken out of the way, moved aside. What is really being said is that, for the first time since creation, sin will be totally unrestrained in the earth. No wonder there will be great tribulation.[1]

To gain a better understanding of what Paul is speaking of in verse seven, we can learn from the example of the natural process which causes a pregnant woman to go into labor.

Scripture compares the last days of the earth to the birth pains of a woman. By understanding the birth process of a child, we can gain insight into the sequence of events which will transpire at the end of the age. Many people are not aware that the body of the mother tries to expel the fetus from the earliest stages of pregnancy. To prevent premature birth, her body produces a hormone which helps to maintain pregnancy and suppress uterine contractions. This process is called the *uterine brake*. In other words, the hormone her body excretes puts brakes on the birth process until the fetus is mature. The mother will not go into labor until the level of this hormone in her blood dramatically decreases. The decrease of this hormone is called the *releasing of the uterine brake*.

Once the hormone quits restraining the labor process, the body of the mother immediately lunges into a painful crescendo of climatic contractions.

Once labor begins, there are three stages of the delivery process that follow. These are:

1. dilation stage

2. expulsion phase

3. expelling the placenta

The releasing of the uterine brake is a perfect parallel to the removing of the restraining force that Paul speaks of in 2 Thess. 2:7. The earth has had false labor pains from the day that sin was conceived in the heart of Eve. There has always been war, and rumors of war, as men have striven for power and peace. Nevertheless, the earth has not yet experienced the effects of unrestrained sin. A time is coming, however, when the Holy Spirit of God will quit restraining sin and will allow it to manifest itself without restraint.

The antichrist will be the full embodiment of unrestrained sin. Like the releasing of the uterine brake in a pregnant woman, his revealing will cause the earth to plunge into intense labor such as the world has never known. The earth will experience great upheavals in humanity as it begins to dilate for the harvest of the two mysteries within the womb. It will be a time of *great tribulation*.

4
Man of Sin

Let no man deceive you by any means: for that day [coming of the Lord and our gathering to Him] shall not come, except there come a falling away first, and that man of sin [antichrist] be revealed, the son of perdition.

(2 Thess. 2:3)

Our hope is built on the redemptive work of the Lord Jesus Christ, the resurrection of the beloved and the promise of His literal return to reign as the Prince of peace. However, we are responsible to prepare ourselves so we will recognize the imposter who will masquerade himself as God before the nations of the earth. He will be the full representation of the seed of deception (tare), as Jesus is the full representation of the seed of truth (wheat). He will be the prince of the mystery of confusion and fear, as Jesus is the Prince of understanding and peace. He will imitate Christ in every way; yet, he will be a deceiver.

Like the releasing of the uterine brake in the woman with child, the Spirit of God will quit restraining the mystery of iniquity and allow it to reveal the wicked one. He will be an abomination to the Holy One. He is the antichrist, and he will so persuasively deceive the nations that the whole world will go after him in a fervent heat.

This chapter is dedicated to providing a knowledge of the antichrist so that we will not be deceived by his powerful persuasions. Instead, as this age draws to a close and the intensity of unstable world conditions increase, we will see God's Word being fulfilled and will be encouraged to lift our heads, knowing His redemption draws nigh.

The antichrist will appear as an angel of light, the answer man, solving riddles of unstable world conditions that have existed for centuries. His brilliant oratory will soothe the nations, but the motivations of his heart will be treacherously wicked. With skilled intrigue and shrewdness he will intimidate and trample all who stand in his way. He will be empowered by the wicked one, Satan, and will continue to increase in arrogance until he is destroyed by the coming of the Lord Jesus (2 Thess. 2:8). Nevertheless, the nations will joyfully receive him with open arms, rejoicing with the hope of peace that he will offer. He will win their confidence.

His Character

The clearest picture of the character of the antichrist is given in the book of Daniel. Daniel writes: "And in the latter time of their kingdom, when the transgressors are come to the full, a king of fierce countenance, and understanding dark sentences, shall stand up. And his power shall be mighty, but not by his own power; and he shall destroy wonderfully, and shall prosper, and practise, and shall destroy the mighty and the holy people. And through his policy also he shall cause craft to prosper in his hand; and he shall magnify himself in his heart, and by peace shall destroy many: he shall also stand up against the Prince of princes; but he shall be broken without hand'' (Dan. 823–25).

In order that we might clearly understand these three verses, let us break them down, list, and define each phrase:

(1) "Fierce countenance"—an insolent, dominating personality; overbearing, powerful, greedy.

(2) "Understanding dark sentences"—the word "dark" means a proverb or riddle; hence, he will have insight far superior to that of the natural man.

(3) "Power shall be mighty, but not his own"—He shall be empowered by Satan (see Rev. 13:14, 15).

(4) "He shall destroy wonderfully"—his ability to defeat and obtain both militarily and through manipulation will be brilliant, extraordinary.

(5) "Shall prosper and practise"—he will push forward, achieve, accomplish, be industrious.

(6) "Destroy the mighty and holy people"—no one will be able to withstand him; he will *eliminate all opposition* (this is probably a direct reference to the destruction of the Jews, wherein two-thirds will be killed—Zech. 13:8, 9). Also, the persecution of the

saints who are the mighty and holy people of God
(Dan. 7:21).

(7) "Through his policy"—discretion, understanding, tactics, wisdom, and prudence.

(8) He "shall cause craft to prosper" ("craft" means deceit or guile)—he shall be brilliantly deceptive.

(9) "Magnify himself in his heart"—here we see the full manifestation of pride, which caused the fall of Lucifer; hence the fall of man ("I will be like the most High"—Isa. 14:14; "ye shall be as gods"—Gen. 3:5).

(10) "And by peace shall destroy many"—this is the worst of all his deceptions. The world will follow him to its destruction, believing he holds the keys to peace.

In this passage, we are shown the full embodiment of all of the attitudes and acts that characterize this man. He is total opposition to the standards of God. He is naked sin, unrestrained—the epitome of all that is the antichrist; a man of pride, posing as a god of light.

His Kingdom

The vehicle he will use to achieve world power will be a latter-day kingdom that is comprised of ten nations emerging out of the old Roman empire (Dan. 7:7, 8, 19–24). It appears as though the European Economic Community (Common Market) meets all of the biblical qualifications required of that kingdom.

If the European Common Market is the ten-nation confederacy spoken of by Daniel, we are indeed approaching the climax of this age. The next move we should be watching for is the rise of a powerful political figure within the confederacy and the eventual subduing of three of the "ten kings" within the system (Dan. 7:8, 24). This power play will expose, for the first time, the prince of darkness manifested in the flesh. He will rise up and usurp control over three of the member nations, causing the other seven to voluntarily submit.

I am not certain what method the antichrist will employ when he makes his initial power play and moves into a position of leadership. The word "subdue" (Dan. 7:24) is, in the original text, "shelf-al," which means "to abase or humble." If one were to mix a bit of theory with the facts we have been given, he or she would deduce that the antichrist will publicly humiliate three of the ten leaders in the Common Market, solving political complications that they are unable to solve. He will use difficult situations to demonstrate that his abilities are by far superior to theirs, thereby leveraging himself (with their vulnerability to peer pressure), and taking control over their positions of authority. He will then display such wisdom that the rest of the world's leaders will be unable to dispute his logic. They will eventually find themselves looking to him for solutions to problems that have remained unresolved throughout history.

Once he has gained control of the ten nations, he will make a seven-year convenant with Israel. The antichrist will be the first man with the capacity to reason with the Jews and bring them into a covenant. This achievement will increase his world prominence. The signing of the convenant is the timepiece that will actually begin the last seven years of this age, which will be concluded by the coming of the Lord! (Dan. 9:27).

His Plan & Timing

We do not know exactly what the covenant will be. However, it is probable that it will in some way relate to the Jewish temple. Isaiah prophesied that this covenant will be a covenant with death. The leaders of Israel will view it as a refuge and a guarantee against destruction. They will be deceived, however, and eventually Israel will be trodden down by the one they have entered into covenant with (Isa. 28;14–18).

Their trusting in him is the fulfillment of the prophecy of Jesus, who said, "I [the true Christ] am come in my Father's name, and ye receive me not; if another [the antichrist] shall come in his own name, him ye will receive" (John 5:43).

The antichrist will betray the Jews in the midst of the seven-year covenant. He will then cause the sacrifice and oblation to cease when he stands in the holy place and declares himself to be God.

It is a common misconception that the great tribulation is a seven-year time period. It is true that this covenant between Israel and the antichrist will mark the beginning of the last seven years of this age. The covenant, however, does *not* mark the beginning of the great tribulation. *The great tribulation does not last for seven years!* Matthew 24:15–21 tells us that the great tribulation will begin after the man of sin proclaims himself to be God in the Holy place, desecrating the

Temple and breaking covenant with the Jews. Daniel 9:27 states that this will take place in the *middle* of the seven-year covenant, and *not* at the beginning. This will leave about three-and-one-half years remaining for the world to experience the great tribulation. It will be a holocaust of unrestrained sin that will burst into a frenzy, to be concluded by the coming of the Lord.

Daniel was very specific about the exact number of days the antichrist would be alloted to masquerade as God on the earth. He stated that from the time the antichrist defiled the Holy Place (by declaring himself to be God) there would be 1,290 days alloted (Dan. 12:11). The 1,290 days of great tribulation will be concluded by the literal return of the Lord Jesus Christ. Jesus will then slay the antichrist with the breath of his mouth, and the splendor of His coming (2 Thess. 2:8; Rev. 19:19).

From the time the antichrist moves into power, things will get progressively worse for those who are devoted to Christ. But after he breaks covenant with Israel, magnifying himself as God in the Holy Place, the time of great tribulation will begin. He will then make it mandatory for all who dwell on the earth to worship him (Rev. 13:8).

The Scripture tells us that the world will worship the antichrist, saying, "Who is like unto the beast? who is able to make war with him?" (Rev. 13:4). He will speak great things and blasphemies; and power will be given unto him to continue forty and two months (three-and-one-half years). He will open his mouth in blasphemy against God—to blaspheme His name, and His tabernacle and them that dwell in heaven. It will be given unto him to make war with the saints and to overcome them: Power will be given to him over all kindreds, tongues, and nations. And all that dwell upon the earth shall worship him, whose names are not written in the book of life of the Lamb slain from the foundation of the world (Rev. 13:5-8).

Once he defiles the Holy Place, it will be open season on every man, woman, or child who refuses to worship him. Like Nimrod, he will be a great hunter. It is interesting that all of the world will worship him *except* those whose names are written in the Lamb's book of life (Rev. 13:8). *Certainly, that exception would not be there if it were not for the Church's continued residence on the earth.*

His Headwound & Despotism

His moving into the Holy Place will most likely be in conjunction with a head wound which he will receive. In Rev. 13:3-5, the events are listed in this order:

(1) head wound

(2) healing

(3) worship of him [he is not actually worshiped worldwide until he stands in the Holy Place and proclaims himself to be God]

(4) blasphemes God forty-two months [three-
and-one-half years—42 lunar months equal
1,260 days]

The antichrist will function as a brilliant leader for
the first half of his seven-year covenant with Israel.
Then, in the middle of the "week" (of years), he will
be wounded with a head wound that will be unques-
tionably lethal. His miraculous recovery will do two
things! (1) It will cause the world to marvel at him,
thereby taking up his defense; and (2) it will give him
the credibility he needs to proclaim himself to be God.

Zechariah gives us a more detailed look at the wound
received by the antichrist. The prophet states that both
his right arm and his right eye will be rendered useless,
and refers to him as the "idol [not idle] shepherd,"
agreeing with Rev. 13:8 that he will be worshiped (Zech.
11:16–17).

Zechariah also states that the antichrist will leave the
flock. This *may* imply that he once walked with Christ,
as did Judas. And he could, quite possibly, be well
known for his knowledge of the Bible. Having a
knowledge of the Bible would give him the credibility
he would need to distort or appear to discredit the
Scriptures. If, at one point in his life, he does walk with
Christ, then the loss of his right eye is, possibly, symbolic of his loss of divine spiritual insight; and the loss
of his arm is, possibly, symbolic of his eventual defeat.
However, it is reasonably clear that the head wound
the antichrist will receive is a literal wound that will
cause the physical loss of those two members of his
body.

When the antichrist is healed from his head wound, he will gain the support of the vast majority of the world. He will then attempt to eliminate the nation of Israel forever. The Jews will then flee for their lives into the wilderness for the three-and-one-half years of great tribulation. The antichrist will seek to destroy them by casting water "out of his mouth," as a flood (Rev. 12:13–17).

Whether or not this is literal water, this writer does not pretend to know. There are other places in Scripture where the word "flood" is used to figuratively portray an army. The earth, however, will swallow the flood, possibly with an earthquake or sandstorm.

The remnant of Jews who escape the wrath of the antichrist will then be out of his reach. Frustrated, he will then focus his attention on the remnant of their seed—those which *keep* the commandments of God and have the testimony of Jesus Christ (Rev. 12:17).

The remnant of the seed of Israel that Jesus speaks of in Rev. 12:17 is the Church. (The seed of Israel is the Word of God [Jesus—Gal. 3:16], and the fruit of that seed is the Church.) By this time, only a remnant of that seed will be left on the earth.

The antichrist will then make war with the remaining saints of God and overcome them. Power will be given to him over all kindreds, tongues, and nations. All that dwell upon the earth shall worship him except God's devoted saints (Rev. 13:7, 8). Unless those days should be shortened, there should no flesh be saved: but for the sake of the elect (the Church), those days shall be shortened (Matt. 24:22).

This will be the most horrible time in all of history.

We are told, in 2 Thess. 2:7, 8, that the force which has restrained the forces of darkness will be removed or set aside in order that wickedness may be revealed, without restraint or limit, embodied in the man of sin—the antichrist.

For those who abide in Christ, this will be a time of abiding confidence as we witness the earth laboring to give birth to the new age of peace and the coming of the Lord.

The prophet Haggai prophesied that God would shake all nations and then the desire of all nations would come (Hag. 2:7). The desire of all nations is peace, and the Prince of peace is Jesus! Although the world does not know it, the desire of all nations is Jesus.

Whether or not we, as individuals, survive in our disposable containers of flesh for the full duration of the tribulation (1,260 days) does not matter; in the end, all who overcome will be with our Lord, and His dominion will be everlasting. Praise His name!

In Summary

In summary, I would like to list the sequence of events that we are to be looking for:

(1) A rising of ten nations out of the old Roman empire (Dan. 2; 7:7, 8, 24). This was probably fulfilled on January 1, 1981, by the formal ratification of the tenth nation—to the European Common Market—Greece.

Note: Although the European Common Market has the appearance of the prophesied latter day 10 nation kingdom, it will take time to unveil the truth as to its actual role in history. Remember, we are exhorted to watch for the signs of the TIMES, but we must be careful not to presume the outcome of events before they occur.

(2) A subduing of three kings of the ten-nation confederacy by a brilliant political leader (the antichrist) as he moves into a position of world leadership (Dan. 7:24). This prophecy should be fulfilled next.

(3) The signing of a seven-year covenant between Israel and this leader (Dan. 9:27, Isa. 28:14–18).

(4) The antichrist will receive a head wound (Zech. 11;16, 17; Rev. 13:3).

(5) He will be miraculously healed—either prevented from dying or raised from death (Rev. 13:3).

(6) He will probably be left with a crippled right eye and arm, although this crippling may be merely symbolic of a spiritual death (Zech. 11:17).

(7) He will move into the holy place and proclaim himself to be God (2 Thess. 2:4; Dan. 12:11; Matt. 24:15).

(8) He will attempt to annihilate the Jews (Rev. 12:13).

(9) Frustrated by his failure to totally obliterate Israel, he will turn his attention to the destruction of Christians (Rev. 12:17).

(10) The whole unredeemed world will worship him for three-and-one-half years (Rev. 13:4, 5).

The following Bible verses are suggested reading: Num. 24:17; Isa. 16:4–14; Dan. 2:35, 44; 7:13, 14, 21–27; Rev. 2:7, 11, 17, 26, 38; 3:5, 12, 21. Reading these verses will provide a clearer perspective on what the Bible says about the last days.

5
The Falling Away

Let no man deceive you by any means: for that day [coming of the Lord and our gathering to Him] shall not come, except there come a falling away first, and that man of sin be revealed, the son of perdition. (2 Thess. 2:3)

To say that the Lord could come at any moment is a statement made at the expense of sound scriptural doctrine. It is of utmost importance that we prepare ourselves to both *expect* and *recognize* the "falling away" of professing belivers first. Paul boldly states that this must take place before the church is gathered.

The word used in the original Greek text—that has been translated "falling away" in the King James Version—is *apostasia*. It means to commit apostasy, to forsake, separate, divorce, or defect from the truth. It does not mean "backslidden, but still under grace." It is a total severing of the relationship.

The Holy Spirit clearly states that, in later times, some will *abandon* the faith and follow deceiving spirits and things taught by demons (1 Tim. 4:1). The church has never been more vulnerable to a mass abandonment of the faith than it is now.

Many of our local church fellowships are being sustained through tradition, while the hearts of the people grow colder. The Word of God has ceased to be personally adhered to by a vast majority of our religious leaders, resulting in a compromise of moral integrity.

Our improper teaching of the Word of God has produced an undisciplined church. It is overflowing with men and women who have *not* been trained in the Lordship of Jesus Christ. They do not know that the New Testament calls Jesus "Savior" only twenty-four times, while He is called "Lord" 703 times. Consequently, we have produced a generation of people who view Jesus as a "fire-insurance policy."

We have taught many of our new converts to ask Jesus to be Savior of their lives, so that they might reap the benefits of being a Christian. Yet we do not teach them the high price of laying down their lives in repentance and submitting in obedience to His Word. Consequently, we have a vast amount of people who accept the fact that Jesus died for the sins of the world; but acceptance without true repentance and submission to His lordship bears no fruit. The tree that bears no fruit will be cut down (see Luke 3:9; John 15:1–6).

There is also a strong trend in the contemporary church to read His Word to acquire knowledge. The motivation within the hearts of many of us has been to be well versed in biblical doctrine in order that we might use our knowledge competitively as an instrument of status, rather than as a vehicle to conform us to the image of our Lord.

My concern is that a lukewarm attitude, coupled with the assertive teaching that Christ is going to remove us before the great tribulation, has caused a vast majority of the now professing Christians to *not* recognize, nor to be concerned with, the "signs of the times." They will *not* recognize the antichrist. Being convinced that the saints will be removed before he comes on the scene, they will receive him as an angel of light. And they will be overwhelmed by his miraculous power. When this happens, their hearts will be deceived and confused by men who herald the antichrist as the savior of the world. These men will be the latter-day scoffers that Peter said will rise up and seek to discredit the gospel of Jesus Christ.

Peter stated that these scoffers would be men walking after their own lusts (2 Peter 3:3–4). If Matt. 24:12 is correct in predicting that iniquity shall abound in the last days, then certainly these men will proclaim the pleasures of a life style that has no boundaries. They will surely seek to discredit the Scripture as erroneous by asking, "Where is the promise of his coming? for since the fathers fell asleep, all things continue as they were from the beginning of creation" (2 Pet. 3:4).

The pressure which will be put on professing believers, who are not abiding in the Lordship of Christ, will be more than they can bear. Many will succumb to the luring of pleasures and pressures of a sin-sick society, falling away from their first love. They will be like those spoken of in the parable of the sower—who received the seed of the Word of God in stony hearts. Having first received it with joy, they will yield to the pressures of society because they have not grounded themselves in Christ. By and by, they will fall away.

After these men and women willingly become ignorant of God and reject the cost of bearing the cross of Jesus to pursue their own lust (2 Peter 3:5), their minds will be darkened with confusion, and they will begin to betray the devoted saints whose purity intimidates them.

There are two different conditions of the Lord's servants at His coming that are demonstrated in Luke 12:42–47. The only servant mentioned as being surprised by the coming of the Lord is the one who is persecuting the other servants. The key to the whole passage in Luke, however, is in verse 45: "If that servant shall say in his heart, My Lord delayeth His coming."

Here, again, we see portrayed the heart of a professing servant of God who does not truly love Jesus or His people. He is not aware of the times, and is indifferent in his affections. When it becomes too inconvenient to maintain a mask of Christianity, then he will turn on the ones who are truly devoted to the Lord— "falling away" from the faith. Jesus says that he will be appointed his portion with the unbelievers, and that his portion would be greater than the unbelievers.

Scripture teaches that once a man has escaped the pollutions of the world through the knowledge of the Lord and Savior Jesus Christ, and is again entangled therein (and is overcome), the latter end is worse with him than the beginning. For it would have been better for him not to have known the way of righteousness, than, after he had known it, to turn from the holy commandment delivered unto him. But it is happened unto him according to the true proverb, "The dog is turned to his own vomit again; and the sow that was washed to her wallowing in the mire" (2 Peter 2:20–22).

We need to pursue the person of Jesus Christ, learning what it means to abide in Him, and how to find in Him a refuge from deceit and destruction.

Look around; the world is in drastic need of answers. The Scriptures say that someone will rise up who will appear to have the answers. The Bible calls him "the ungodly man of sin." As he begins to unite the world, and soothe it with his brilliant oratory, he will also begin to *magnify himself*. He will impose systems and strategies that will, at first, appear to be the answers to the world's unsettled conditions. All will be deceived, except for God's very elect.

As Christians refuse to yield to his demands, the world will view them as opposers of world peace and a threat to its security.

At first, demands will be small. Then they will become more intense (as in Hitler's Germany). Initially, his systems will be optional; however, more and more pressure will be put on everyone to conform until everything climaxes by his desecration of the Temple and his proclamation that he is God (2 Thess. 2:4; Matt. 24:15).

At this point, it will be mandatory that we receive his number or mark—signifying that we worship him as God. This will be easy for the unredeemed to do, because to them he will appear to be of God. They will be deceived by his power and the miracles he performs.

The price of being a Christian will be so high that

there will no longer be any room for the spiritually lukewarm. The mandatory mark will conclude a great spiritual exodus of lukewarm Christians, so that none will remain, except those who love Christ more than their own lives.

those who follow him have the blessings of God. He will easily be able to persuade them, as he appeases their conscience by appearing to be of God, while at the same time offering a permissive outlook toward pursuing the desires of the flesh. In other words, those who follow him will be able to have their cake and eat it, too.

The antichrist will so sway the nations that men will seek to purge the world of those who oppose him. They will believe in their hearts (as Saul did in the book of Acts) that they are serving God by destroying Christians (see John 16:2).

According to 2 Thess. 2:7, this will be a time when the force that has restrained the powers of darkness will quit restraining and will step aside. This will allow the mature fruit of the seed of pride and confusion (first sown in the garden of Eden) to raise its ugly head and demonstrate to all of the heavenly principalities its need for judgment and destruction.

It will also be a time of perfecting, purging, and preparing the bride of Christ, so that she can stand maturely in the earth—a final and glorious demonstration of the love of God to all who dwell on the earth and in the heavenlies.

After all of the purposes of God have been fulfilled and the great tribulation draws to a close, the mystery of God (the good fruit of the earth—the Church) will be ready for harvest. Christians will *then* be removed from the earth in order that *God's wrath* might be executed, destroying those who destroy the earth (Rev. 11:18).

It will be just like the days of Noah and Lot; the righteous are removed for preservation and the wicked are brought to judgment within the same day. May the Lord Jesus be glorified in our devotion to Him!

6
The Great Tribulation

In natural childbirth, the releasing of the uterine brake begins the *dilation stage*. The dilation stage is the first stage of labor which enlarges the birth canal to prepare it for the passage of the baby. This process of enlarging the birth canal is a series of rhythmic contractions that become increasingly intense and painful. The dilation stage must be completed before the expulsion of the baby will begin.

Like the dilation stage, the great tribulation will be a time of extremely painful, uncontrollable upheavals of humanity. Men will be laboring in their own strength to give birth to the elusive desire of peace; however, conditions will only intensify until the earth peaks in unbearble chaos.

Until the Holy Spirit of God quits restraining the powers of darkness and allows the antichrist to be revealed, the striving of humanity will be comparably mild, as are the false labor ("Braxton Hicks") contractions. But, like the releasing of the uterine brake, the Spirit of God will quit restraining the powers of darkness, releasing the seed of the mystery of confusion (tare) to bring forth its ripened fruit—the antichrist. He will arouse the nations to a crescendo of un-precedented confusion.

What is the Tribulation?

The word from the original Greek, which has been translated "tribluation" in Scripture, is *Thlipsis*. It means to be in affliction, anguish or persecution. *Contrary to popular belief, there are no places, within the Scriptures that state or imply, that the great tribulation is the wrath of God in the earth. Rather, it is a time of great affliction and tribulation.* The wrath of God will occur immediately after the tribulation (Matt. 24:29), as we will see in the following chapters.

The tribulation is a time when God will allow the two mysteries of the earth to come into maturity. The church will be mature, corporately demonstrating the fullness of the seed of truth in the earth (the wheat). And the antichrist will be the full personification of the powers of darkness, demonstrating the fullness of the seed of deception in the earth (the tare). The conflict of the two forces, as they collide, will bring about great tribulation for three-and-one-half years (which is the same amount of time that was alloted for the ministry of Jesus).

When and How Long Is the Tribulation?

The great tribulation period is not seven years long! Jesus referred to the prophecies of Daniel, stating that the great tribulation would begin when the antichrist defiled the holy place (Matt. 24:15, 21). Daniel prophesied that the antichrist would stand in the holy place and defile it in the middle of the last seven years (Dan. 9:27). This tells us that we will have approximately three-and-one-half years from the signing of the seven-year covenant between Israel and the antichrist until the tribulation begins. *This would leave about three-and-one-half years remaining for the time period defined as the great tribulation.*

The antichrist will have total dominion over the earth for the full three-and-one-half years of the tribulation period. Daniel states that, from the time the abomination (the antichrist) is set up (defiling the holy place), there shall be 1,290 more days of his reign. (Dan. 12:11) His reign will be terminated by the coming of the Lord (2 Thess. 2:8).

Six major episodes of the great tribulation are presented in Scripture. These will last for the full duration of the three-and-one-half years of tribulation. They are:

1. The holy city of Jerusalem will be tread underfoot by the gentiles for forty-two months—three-and-one-half years (1260 days)—(Rev. 11:2, 12:7–13; Matt. 24:15).

2. The surviving Jews will flee into the wilderness to be nourished by God from the face of the serpent for a time, and times, and a half a time—three-and-one-half years (1260 days)—(Rev. 12:14).

3. The Church will endure extreme persecution as the antichrist prevails against them for "a time and times and the dividing of time"—three-and-one-half years (1260 days)—(Dan. 7:21, 25; Dan. 12:6–7; Rev. 12:17; Rev. 13:5–7).

4. Men will worship the dragon (antichrist) for forty-two months—three-and-one-half years (1260 days)—(Rev. 13:4–8).

5. The antichrist will blaspheme God, and His tabernacle (Church), and all them that dwell in heaven, for forty-two months—three-and-one-half years (1260 days)—(Rev. 13:5–6).

6. God will empower two witnesses to prophesy against the antichrist and his cohorts for 1260 days—three-and-one-half years—(Rev. 11:3).

When the antichrist defiles the holy place and declares himself to be God, he will establish Jerusalem as his seat and as the center of world dominion. The gentile armies that he commands will tread the holy city underfoot, and he will deceitfully establish himself as the Messiah that was prophesied to rule the world from Jerusalem.

When he desecrates the holy place, the Jews will then realize that they have made a drastic mistake by trusting him. They will flee for their lives into the wilderness, and the fortunate ones will barely escape his intense persecution.

Frustrated by his failure to totally destroy the Jews, he will turn his fury toward the remnant of the seed of Israel (Rev. 12:17). The seed of Israel is Christ (Gal. 3:16), and the remnant of Christ that is in the earth is His Church.

The antichrist will demand that all men worship him universally and receive the mark of the number of his name (Rev. 13:16–18). He will begin to blaspheme God and His tabernacle and those who dwell in the heavens. He will also raise up a false prophet who will have the appearance of a lamb, but who will speak as a dragon. The false prophet will exercise all of the power of the antichrist and will cause the earth (and them which dwell therein) to worship him. He will do great wonders, so that he will make fire come down from heaven to the earth in the sight of men. And the miracles he will perform will deceive all who dwell on the earth, except for those whose names are written in the Lamb's Book of Life.

The false prophet will convince those who dwell on the earth that they should make an image of the antichrist. He will then use his great power to bring the image to life, so that the image will be able to speak. The image will cause all who will not worship the false prophet to be killed (Rev. 13:4-15). This will be a time of bloodshed such as the world has never witnessed. Men will betray close members of their own families out of their blind loyalty to that unholy beast. The hearts of men will harden so that they will perform feats of cruelty unsurpassed in the history of the world.

In the opening verses of the eleventh chapter of the book of Revelation, John is told by the angel of the Lord to go and measure the Temple of God. All of God's Word teaches us that the true Temple of God is the Church.[1]

At the beginning of the tribulation, the Temple of God (the Church) will be measured (see Rev. 11:1). The

Church will be found to be mature, walking with God (as was Enoch). It will be ready for harvest. Then, the Lord will raise two witnesses to represent the Church before the nations during the tribulation period (Rev. 11:3).

These events were foreshadowed in the Old Testament by the nation of Israel. Israel (God's people) grew into maturity in Egypt (a land of bondage). In Exod. 3:7-10, we see that God visited Israel and determined that they were ready for deliverance. He then raised two witnesses (Moses and Aaron), who confronted Pharoah (and his masters of the black arts). There, they met occult opposition from the Egyptians (as will the two witnesses described in Rev. 11). However, as the authority of Moses and Aaron was superior to that of the sorcerers of Egypt, so the authority of the two witnesses will be superior to that of the antichrist and his false prophet.

Like Moses and Aaron, these two witnesses will represent God and His people to the nations. They will prophesy against the ungodly, shut up the rain, and call plagues upon the earth for three-and-one-half years (Rev. 11:3-6). They will probably release the first six (of seven) trumpet plagues, which are recorded in chapters eight and nine of the book of Revelation. God did not allow Pharaoh or the Egyptians to hurt Moses or Aaron. In like manner, no one will be allowed to hurt these two witnesses until they have *finished* their testimony.

We must remember that Israel was not allowed to leave Egypt instantly. Rather, they remained under ever-increasing persecution from the hands of Pharaoh.

But, while Pharaoh was making life difficult for the Jews, God was bringing plagues upon the Egyptians through the hands of Moses and Aaron. The plagues that were brought on Egypt had no effect on Israel. And so will it be with the Church in the last days of this age; the plagues called to earth by the two witnesses will have no effect on God's people.

As it was in Egypt, the persecution of the beloved by the hand of the antichrist will grow in intensity, and the two witnesses will be used of God to bring ever increasing plagues upon those who dwell on the earth. The people of the earth will hate the two witnesses, and will accuse them of being the ones who torment the earth (Rev. 11:10). This is the same accusation that Ahab made to Elijah (see 1 Kings 18:17, 18)—"You who troubles Israel." These people (as did Ahab), speak out of hearts hardened by the deceitfulness of sin. In each situation, the cause of the torment is not the prophet of God, but the sin of the people.

Sin's devastation will drive God's people further and further into His arms, until at last, like Israel, the Church will make an exodus from this land of bondage (the earth) to receive her promised inheritance (which is the literal presence of God and the unlimited infilling of His Spirit).

The people of Israel had to have their hearts purged of Egypt in the wilderness. They needed to be circumcised of the flesh before they were ready to possess the promised inheritance of God (Josh. 5:2-9). Likewise, the church will go through a period of intense purging, removing those branches that bear no fruit (the great falling away). Those who remain will be circumcised of the desires of the flesh so that they will stand with a singleness of eye, a righteous and glorious demonstration of the character of our Lord.

In the final days, the Church will stand as did Israel, gazing from the wilderness side of the Jordan river, across its banks to the promised inheritance of the Lord's coming. We will go through the last three-and-one-half years of sin's unrestrained dominion, as a people comparable to the men of valor of David's throne. Christians will do exploits (Dan. 11:32), performing glorious demonstrations of the fearlessness of the Lion of our tribe. Although many of them will experience physical destruction, their spirits will be unquenchable testimonies of Shiloh (Jesus), whose scepter shall rule the nations, and shall not depart.

The man whose loyalty is to the true God will have a personal escort through the furnace of affliction by our Lord Jesus, the Son of God (Dan. 3:25). The man who loves God with a pure heart will not dwell in fear during the tribulation (Dan. 3:16–18), but will give himself freely in the day of God's power, in the beauty of holiness (Ps. 110:3). He will not be afraid though ten thousands of people should set themselves against him round about, for the Lord our God is a shield to those who love Him. He is their glory, and the lifter of their heads.

As the church comes into maturity, corporately demonstrating the Word of God in the earth, we will overcome our inner man by the power of God's Word and by the blood of the Lamb. *The greatest conflict we will ever experience is not the great tribulation, but rather the conflict that rages in the innermost sanc-*

tuaries of our heart and mind. If a man gains victory over his flesh and is conformed to the image of Christ in his heart, then any external conflict that may be hurled at him by a sin-sick society will be easy for him to endure.

When the fruit of the earth becomes ripe, the Son of man will prepare to send His angels forth to harvest the earth. The tares will be gathered in bundles to be burned first, and the wheat will be gathered into the barn where they will shine like the sun in the kingdom of their Father (Matt. 13; James 5:7).

7
The Expulsion Phase

When the dilation of the birth canal is complete, the *expulsion phase* begins.

The expulsion phase is the process of actually expelling the infant from the body. It is a relatively brief, yet intense stage of labor. Rupture of the amniotic sack (water breaking) generally occurs at the beginning of this stage. The contractions then become methodical and severe as the child begins his journey through the birth canal. Once the child enters the canal, the mother will find that she is unable to refrain from pushing. She will experience feelings of desperation as she finds herself no longer in control. The seed that has been sown in her womb, and nurtured to maturity, is about to be harvested—thus fullfilling the law of sowing and reaping.

And so it is with the earth. There are two seeds that have been sown in its womb. Like the seeds in the womb of Rebekah (Jacob and Esau), these are two nations, two manner of people, that are struggling against one another for the inheritance of the earth. The first is a nation that is called out and chosen, and has received and nurtured with endurance the engrafted Word of God. The second is a nation that has received and nurtured the seed of the tare, esteeming the pottage of the earth as greater riches than the birthright that was purchased by the blood of Christ.

Immediately *after the tribulation* (the dilation stage), the two seeds (of the wheat and the tare) will begin to be harvested (beginning the expulsion phase). The remnant of the seed of Christ will have ripened to understanding and complete trust in God, and will then be harvested into His presence. Meanwhile, the seed of deception will have matured to absolute confusion and fear, and will be harvested into bundles in the valley of Armageddon for the outpouring of God's burning wrath.

After the church is removed, the kingdoms of the earth will experience intense desperation. Like a woman in the expulsion stage of labor, they will realize that they are no longer in control. Confusion and fear will dominate their minds, so that their hearts will fail. There will be signs in the sun, and in the moon, and in the stars; and upon the earth will come distress of nations, with perplexity; the sea and the waves will roar in response to the catastrophic condition of the earth. They will be consumed with fear in their innermost beings, for the powers of heaven shall be shaken (Matt. 24:29; Luke 21:25, 26).

There is an event that *briefly precedes* the harvest of the church. This event will tell those who are watching that the tribulation period is finished, and that the wheat and the tare are about to be harvested. That event is the slaying of the two witnesses.

The two witnesses will be untouchable until they finish their testimonies. However, once the three-and-one-half years of tribulation is complete, and their three-and-one-half years of prophesying in sackcloth have been fulfilled, the antichrist will be allowed to make war with them and kill them (Rev. 11:7).

Their dead bodies will then be displayed in the streets of Jerusalem for three-and-one-half days. And all of the people and nations, and those who dwell on the earth, will rejoice over their destruction, exchanging gifts and making merry because these two prophets (which have tormented them) have been slain (Rev. 11:10).

The world will believe that the slaying of the two witnesses will bring peace and safety at last. It will rejoice in their destruction, convinced that this is an end of the plagues and persecutions that they have brought on the earth. It will also believe that this victory is a final demonstration of the omnipotence of their false god—the antichrist.

They will be terribly deceived, because this is the time of the fulfilling of the prophecy of Paul: *"For when they shall say, peace and safety; then sudden destruction cometh upon them, as travail upon a woman with child; and they shall not escape"* (1 Thess. 5:3 Italics mine).

Peace and safety will be short-lived! There will be only three-and-one-half days after the death the two witnesses until they will be resurrected and called to heaven. This will cause great fear to fall on all of those who see them (Rev. 11:11). Once the two witnesses are called into the heavens in a cloud, the "third woe" will come quickly (Rev. 11:14).

The third woe is the blowing of the seventh trumpet by the seventh angel. It will initiate the harvest of the Church into God's presence, and the outpouring of God's wrath on the earth. John writes, "When he [the seventh angel] shall begin to sound [the seventh trumpet], the mystery of God should be finished, as he hath declared to his servants the prophets" (Rev. 10:7; 11:15).

The seventh trumpet will announce the completion of the mystery of God—the Church. There are only two series of trumpets recorded in Scripture—at the battle of Jericho and the seven trumpets in the book of Revelation. The seventh (last) trumpet of the Revelation will announce the completion of the mystery of God. It is, therefore, the only "last trumpet" of Scripture that can be related to Paul's prophecy in his first letter to the Corinthian church. "Behold, I shew you a mystery; We shall not all sleep, but we shall all be changed, In a moment, in the twinkling of an eye, *at the last trump*: for the trumpet shall sound, and the dead shall be raised incorruptible, and we shall be changed" (1 Cor. 15:51, 52, italics mine).

Like the seventh trumpet of the battle of Jericho, which foreshadowed this event, the last trumpet (of the seven trumpets fortold in the book of Revelation) will be accompanied by a shout proclaiming that the kingdoms of this world are become the kingdoms of our Lord and His Christ (Rev. 11:15; Josh. 6:20).

The bursting of the amniotic sack, during natural childbirth, generally testifies that the dilation stage has been completed and the expulsion phase has begun. Likewise, the seventh trumpet will announce the expulsion of the two seeds. First, it will proclaim the completion of the Church, initiating its harvest from the earth and, thereby, bringing the servants of all ages into the presence of God to receive their just rewards (Rev. 11:15-18). Second, it will announce the collapse of sin's dominion in the earth. This will initiate the gathering of the tares of all nations to Armageddon to resist the coming of the Lord, and will usher in the wrath of God.

God's wrath will be a time of purging to destroy all who destroy the earth. Destined for destruction are those who worship the beast and his image, and who have received the mark of the number of his name (Rev. 14:9-11). Even after the walls of Jericho fell and the land was given as a possession to Israel, there was a brief work of purging before they occupied it (Rev. 11:18; Josh. 6:21-24).

Jesus said that the harvest of the Church would be like the days of Lot: "The same day that Lot went out of Sodom it rained fire and brimstone from heaven, and destroyed them all" (Luke 17:29).

And so it is with the climax of the age: the seventh trumpet will blow; the wheat will be harvested into the presence of God for preservation, and the tares will be gathered into bundles in the valley of Megiddo (Armageddon), where they will encounter the outpouring of the burning wrath of God.

In Rev. 14:14-20, we are given a detailed account of the two-phase harvest of the wheat and the tare.

The first phase of the harvest is by the Son of man. He will thrust His sickle into the earth and reap the good harvest (which is the wheat), (see vv. 14-16). This is the harvest of the precious fruit of the earth, which the husbandman has had long patience for, waiting to receive both the early and latter rain (see James 5:7). Jesus stated that "when the fruit is brought forth, immediately he putteth in the sickle, because the harvest is come" (Mark 4:29).

The second phase is the harvest of the tare. (See vv. 17–20). It is in conjunction with the harvest of the righteous. The angel will thrust his sickle into the earth and gather the clusters of the vine of the earth. He will then cast them into the great winepress of the wrath of God.

As the fruit of each of the seeds is harvested, the Church will be caught up into the innermost chambers of the heavenly Holy of holies—before the very presence of God for marriage to the Lamb. And the religious whore (Mystery Babylon, which is the mother of pride, the abomination of the earth) is gathered with the king of pride (the antichrist), and her children from all nations. They gather to the valley of Megiddo for the great battle of Armageddon, where they will attempt to resist the coming of the Lord (Rev. 19:19). In this great battle, the Lord Jesus will tread the great winepress of the wrath of God.

Isaiah summed up the whole event in one passage:

Awake and sing, ye that dwell in dust: for thy dew is as the dew of herbs, and the earth shall cast out the dead. [Ressurection]

Come, my people, *enter thou into thy chambers*, and shut thy doors about thee: hide thyself as it is were for a little moment, until the indignation be overpast [the church is brought into the heavenlies for preservation from God's wrath and for marriage to the Lamb].

For, behold, the Lord cometh out of his place *to punish the inhabitants of the earth for their iniquity:* the earth also shall disclose her blood, and shall no more cover her slain.

In that day the Lord with his sore and great and strong sword shall punish leviathan [Satan] the piercing serpent, even leviathan that crooked serpent; and he shall slay the dragon [antichrist] that is in the sea [humanity]. (Isaiah 26:19–27:1, italics mine).

8
The Two-Fold Harvest

The Marriage

The harvest of the Church (Rev. 14:14–16) will bring us into the innermost chambers of the sanctuary of God. Revelation fifteen records the Church (those who have gotten the victory over the beast, over his image, over his mark and over the number of his name) standing on the sea of glass before God's throne in the heavens (Rev. 15:2). We have been brought into the heavenly Holy of holies, before His presence, to partake of the great marriage of supper of the Lamb.

There is much that could be said of the marriage. The bride is the handiwork of the Lord Jesus Christ. He has taken a people destined for destruction and overwhelmed them with His grace so that they have become infatuated with Him. Therefore, His Church has zealously adorned themselves with righteous deeds out of a burning desire to please Him. Like the long awaited arrival of a child, the Church will behold Him face to face, in utter ecstasy.

Jesus will then present us (as a faultless bride) before the presence of the glory of God with exceeding joy

(Jude 24). As the bride is presented before the throne, she will be so overwhelmed by His glory that she will begin to sing the song of Moses, which is a song of victory (Rev. 15:3; Exod. 15:1–21), and the song of the Lamb, magnifying Him as the King of Saints, and His bride will also proclaim in song His right to manifest His judgment toward those who embrace sin (Rev. 15:3–4).

The judgment that Jesus will manifest will be the judgment of the great "whore" that did corrupt the earth (false religions, or tares). From the innermost chambers of the heavenly Holy of holies, the Church will witness the avenging of the righteous servants of God as the wrath of God is poured out upon the earth. God's servants will then understand clearly all that God has done for those who have responded to His grace.

With one voice, the saints of all ages will sing, "Allelujah; Salvation, and glory, and honour, and power, unto the Lord our God: For true and righteous are his judgments: for he hath judged the great whore, which did corrupt the earth with her fornication, and hath avenged the blood of His servants at her hand" (Rev. 19:1–3).

As we repeatedly praise God, the four-and-twenty elders, and the four beasts which stand before the throne of God, will fall prostrate before God and worship Him, saying, "Amen! Allelujah!" (see v. 4). As their praises ring out, a voice will come out of the throne, saying for all of His servants to praise Him (v. 5). Then all of the creation of God (with the bride) as a voice of a great multitude, as the voice of many waters, and as the voice of mighty thundering, will begin to shout, "Allelujah: for the Lord God omnipotent reigneth. Let us be glad and rejoice. . . for the marriage of the Lamb has come, and His wife hath made herself ready" (Rev. 19:4-8).

The Temple of the Holy Spirit (Bride) will be completed at this point. We will then be filled with the glory of the Most High God. Continuous praise will burst forth from the bride, the angelic hosts and all of the myriads of the heavens. This will be a harvest festival so glorious that we will be drunk with the joyous infilling of the Holy Spirit, and so consumed with His glory that we will not be able to stand (as were the priests that forshadowed this event at the dedications of the Solomon's temple—see 2 Chron. 5:13-14). The Temple, (Church, Bride) will be filled with the smoke from the Shekinah Glory of the Most High God, and from His power. He will then fill us to the uttermost with His Spirit without limit—just like our Lord!

The bride will then be honored among the host of heaven, in the presence of the Lamb and the Ancient of Days. We shall be all glorious within, our clothing of wrought gold. We shall be brought unto the King in raiment of needlework (see Ps. 45:14). We will be arrayed in fine linen, clean and white, for the fine linen is the righteousness of the saints.[1]

After we are adorned, Christ will receive us unto himself—a glorious church, not having spot, wrinkle or any such thing; but we will be holy and without blemish (Eph. 5:27).

Then, Christ will move among the midst of His Church, the bride. He will declare the glory of the name of the Most Holy One unto us, singing the praise of

the Ancient of Days in our midst (Heb. 2:12). All of the
universe will stand silently in awe, as the Lord of Glory
lifts His voice in perfect praise. When He completes
His chorus of praise, His saints will be unable to con-
tain themselves, but will burst forth with praise and
and adoration, singing to His delight:

> Thou art fairer than the children of men:
> grace is poured into they lips: therefore God
> hath blessed thee for ever. . . Thou lovest
> righteousness, and hatest wickedness: there-
> fore God, they God, hath anointed thee with
> the oil of gladness above thy fellows. (Ps.
> 45:2, 7)

Being the express image of the perfect love of the
Father, Jesus will then respond to our praises,
delighting in us and singing:

> Rise up, my love, my fair one, and come
> away. For, lo, the winter is past, the rain is
> over and gone; The flowers appear on the
> earth; the time of the singing of birds is come,
> and the voice of the turtle is heard in our
> land. . . Arise, my love, my fair one, and
> come away. (Song of Sol. 2:10–13)

We will be brought into the palace of the King with
gladness and rejoicing (Ps. 45:15). There, Jesus will
partake of the marriage supper of the Lamb with the
saints of all ages—His bride. The ones that He birthed
through the blood and water which flowed from His

side at calvary. We will be like Him, conformed to His image, and a delight to His eyes (as was Eve to Adam's). We will be a reflection of Him, taken from His side at calvary and brought forth through His suffering (wherein He shed His blood for us). Christ is not fulfilled in the fellowship of His creation of the principalities and dominions of the universe but, as was a type in Adam's dilemma, He needed bone of His bone and flesh of His flesh. He desires a companion created in His image (as Eve was in Adam's). We are that nation, His lovely bride! We are the Word of His Word, made in His likeness, birthed through the blood and water that flowed at calvary.

Blessed are they which are called to the marriage supper of the Lamb. They shall sit at table with God and be filled.

Do not neglect so great a salvation. Many are called, but only those who diligently seek Him find Him. Pursue Christ while He may be found, and He will reward you with himself. He's your rock, your fortress, your sure foundation. In Him is peace, and the joy of acceptance. Cease your striving; there is rest in Him.

The true inheritance of Abraham's descendants is recorded in Gen. 15:1. "I am thy shield, and thy exceeding great reward." God has made a covenant to give himself to us, and has sealed it in His own blood!

The Wrath of God

The second phase of the two-fold harvest transpires along with the first (Rev. 14:17-20). It is a harvest for the purpose of gathering the tares to Armageddon for the great winepress of the wrath of God.

Once the good harvest of the earth has been gathered (the wheat), there will be no further reason to allow the earth to remain in its present condition. The clusters of the vine of the earth will begin to be gathered to Armageddon for the final outpouring of God's wrath, where the tares will be burned. This same pattern is demonstrated through the experiences of Lot as he departed Sodom. As Jesus said, "The same day that Lot went out of Sodom it rained fire and brimstone from heaven, and destroyed them all" (Luke 17:29).

Just as chapter fifteen of the book of Revelation gives a detailed account of what happens to those who have been included in the first phase of the harvest (the wheat), chapter sixteen provides a detailed account of what transpires toward those who have embraced wickedness.

Like the company of destroying angels that were sent to Egypt to execute God's fierce wrath (Ps. 78:49), seven angels will be sent to execute the wrath of God in the earth. They will be sent forth out of the Temple (the Church), which is now in heaven, and will pour out the seven vials of the seven last plagues on the earth (Rev. 15:1, 5-7; 16:1).

The seven angels which come out of the Temple are, most likely, the same seven angels, which are the seven stars of the seven churches in the right hand of Christ (Rev. 1:20). They are probably the stars which fall from heaven (Matt. 24:29). One could speculate that these seven personalities would be more than willing to execute the Lord's judgment, after having labored as guardians over the Church for so long—witnessing time and time again the destructive power of the deceptive seed of the tare.

Regardless of who they are, the vials that they pour out on the earth will usher in a period of indescribable chaos. It will be a time when the Temple in heaven will be shut so that *no man will be allowed to enter* to receive of the grace of God and the precious cleansing blood of the Lamb (Rev. 15:8; Isa. 26:20).

During this brief period of time, the men who have worshiped the beast will become covered with loathsome, malignant sores; every living thing in the sea will die as it becomes like the blood of a dead man; the rivers and springs of fresh water will become blood so that men will have nothing but blood to drink. The sun will scorch men with fire, yet they will continue to blaspheme God and will not repent. Darkness will cover the kingdom of the beast, and men will gnaw their tongues because of pain. The great Euphrates river will be dried up, so that the kings of the earth will be able to bring their armies quickly across to be gathered into a place called Armageddon. There will be thunder, and lightning; and a great earthquake—such as has not been since men were first upon the face of the earth; cities of the nations will fall; every island will flee away, and the mountains will not be found; great hailstones will fall from heaven. Yet, men will continue to blaspheme God, for the plague thereof will be exceeding great (Rev. 16).

Isaiah prophesied that the Lord will make the earth empty, wasted, and will turn it upside down and scatter the inhabitants thereof abroad. The earth will mourn and languish, and the haughty people of the earth will languish. Because of their transgressions, the inhabitants of the earth would be burned and *few men would be left*.

Isaiah said that the windows on high will be opened, and the foundations of the earth will be shaken; the earth will be utterly broken, split through, shaken violently; The earth shall reel to and fro like a drunkard, and shall be removed like a cottage; and the transgression thereof shall be heavy upon it; and it shall fall and not rise again. In that day, the Lord shall punish the host of the high ones on high (principalities of darkness), and the kings of the earth upon the earth (see Isa. 24).

Jesus confirmed Isaiah's words, stating that immediately *after* the tribulation of those days God's wrath would be poured out. The sun will be darkened, and the moon shall not give her light, and the stars (the stars represent the seven angels that execute God's wrath—see Rev. 1:20; 16:1) shall fall from heaven. And the powers of heaven (the principalities of darkness) shall be shaken (Matt. 24:29).

In the midst of all of these judgments of God, three unclean spirits like frogs will go forth from the mouth of the dragon, the beast and the false prophet. They are spirits of devils, working miracles, which go forth unto the kings of the earth (and of the whole world). The reason they go forth is to gather the kings, with their armies, together to the battle of that great day of God Almighty (to a place that is called Armageddon in the Hebrew language—see Rev. 16:13-16).

The devil is certainly aware that Jesus is about to take possesion of the earth. Therefore, he gathers the kings of the world by convincing them that they can resist the coming of the Lord Jesus Christ (Rev. 19:19). The gathering of the kings and the beast to Armageddon is the final act of man which ushers in the coming of the Lord (Rev. 16:15).

The day that the Lord returns will be a dreadful day. It is the day of judgment when He treads the winepress of the wrath of God (Amos 5:18; Joel 1:15; 2:1, 2; Mal. 4:1-5; Zeph. 1:7, 14-18; Obad. 15; Rev. 11:18). The brethren are not in darkness that that day should overtake them as a thief, for God has not appointed them to wrath (1 Thess. 5:4, 9).

The prophet Joel summed up the day of the Lord in one proclamation as he cried out:

Proclaim ye this among the Gentiles; Prepare war, wake up the mighty men, let all the men of war draw near; let them come up: Beat your plowshares into swords, and your pruninghooks into spears: let the weak say, I am strong. Assemble yourselves (armies of the Earth), and come, all ye heathen, and gather yourselves together round about: thither cause they mighty ones (Armies of Heaven) to come down, O Lord. Let the heathen be wakened, and come up to the valley of Jehoshaphat: for there will I sit to judge all the heathen round about. Put ye in the sickle, for the harvest is ripe: come, get you down; for the press is full, the fats overflow; for their wickedness is great. Multitudes, multitudes in the valley of decision: for *the day of the Lord* is near in the valley of decision. The sun and the moon shall be darkened, and the stars shall withdraw their shining. The Lord also shall roar out of Zion, and utter his voice from Jerusalem; and the heavens and the earth shall shake: but the Lord will be the hope of his people, and the strength of the children of Israel. (Joel 3:9–16, italics mine).

9
The Day of the Lord

The earth is the promised inheritance of the saints, as Canaan was promised to the nation of Israel (Gen. 15:16; Matt. 5:5; Dan. 7:27). When the marriage of the Lamb and His church is completed in the heavens, the earth will be ready for the final stages of judgment and possession by the saints.

The 1,290 days that were alloted to the man of sin have been fullfilled,[1] and the earth is staggering under the vial judgments which were poured out by the seven angels. The human mind is unable to capture the awesomeness of this moment in the zenith of sin's deception.

The armies of the earth's nations will be gathered in the valley of Armageddon to attempt to thwart the coming of the Lord. They will be dressed in full battle array, yet their inner man will be clothed in uncertainty and confusion; their stomachs will be weak with anxiety, while their arrogant desire to resist God will set the stage for their own destruction. The light of the Word of God has been extinguished in the earth with the removal of the church (the bride) and the nations are blindly committed to the prince of darkness, the antichrist.

As truth has wrought its perfect work in the Church, deception is now having its perfect work in the earth, bringing forth its fruit of confusion, fear, and death.

The nations are being led in vain deception by the three unclean spirits that have come forth out of the mouth of the dragon and the antichrist and his prophet) Rev. 16:13–16). And the kings of the earth are gathered to the valley of Armageddon under the banner of the antichrist, whom they worship as God. They will seek to make war against Christ and His Church (Rev. 17:14; 19:19; Mic. 4:11-13; Ps. 2; Dan. 8:25).

John wrote, "And I saw the beast, and the kings of the earth, and their armies, gathered together to make war against him that sat on the horse [Jesus], and against his army [the church]" (Rev. 19:19).

As the marriage of the Lamb is completed in heaven, we will return with our Lord to execute judgment in a final clash of these two forces (1 Cor. 6:2; Zech. 14:5; Col. 3:4; 1 Thess. 3:13; 1 Thess. 4:14; Jude 14, 15).

As the beast, the kings of the earth and their armies are gathered together to make war against the Lord and His anointed, the heavens will be opened. And as the lightning comes out of the east, and shines even to the west, so shall the coming of the Son of man be.

He and His bride will come as eagles to where the carcase is (Carcase, in Greek, is *pto´-mah*. It means: lifeless body, corpse, antichrist. (See Matt. 24:28). Then, Christ will tread the winepress of the fierceness of His wrath.

John writes:

> And I saw heaven opened, and behold a white horse; and he that sat upon him was called Faithful and True, and in righteousness he doth judge and make war. His eyes were as a flame of fire, and on his head were many crowns; and he had a name written, that no man knew, but he himself. And he was clothed with a vesture dipped in blood: and his name is called The Word of God. And the armies which were in heaven followed him upon white horses, clothed in fine linen, white and clean. And out of his mouth goeth a sharp sword, that with it he should smite the nations: and he shall rule them with a rod of iron: and he treadeth the winepress of the fierceness and wrath of Almighty God. And he hath on his vesture and on his thigh a name written, KING OF KINGS, AND LORD OF LORDS. And I saw an angel standing in the sun; and he cried with a loud voice, saying to all the fowls that fly in the midst of heaven, Come and gather yourselves together unto the supper of the great God; That ye may eat of the flesh of kings, and the flesh of captains, and the flesh of mighty men, and the flesh of horses, and of them that sit on them, and the flesh of all men, both free and bond, both small and great. (Rev. 19:11–18).

The beast and the kings of all nations, and the rest

of their armies, will unite to make war against Him (Jesus) that sits on the horse and against His army (Rev. 19:19). They will be full of rage, vainly imagining that they can withstand the wrath of the Lamb. Taking council together, the kings will say, "Let us break their bands asunder and cast away their cords from us." He that sitteth in the heavens shall laugh; the Lord shall have them in derision. He will speak to them in His wrath and vex them in His sore displeasure (Ps. 2:1–5).

According to the Bible, the Lord shall go forth and fight against those nations, as when He fought in the day of battle (Zech. 14:3): "And it shall come to pass in that day, that a great tumult from the Lord shall be among them; and they shall lay hold every one on the hand of his neighbour, and his hand shall rise up against the hand of his neighbor" (Zech. 14:13).

The tumult that Christ will send among the beast and the kings of all nations will be just like the tumult He sent among the descendents of Ham (the Moabites and the Ammonites) in the battle of Jehoshaphat (described in 2 Chron. 20). As the Moabites sought to destroy Jehoshaphat and the tribe of Judah, they were met by a company of priests out of Judah who were praising the beauty of God's holiness. The Moabites were then consumed with confusion and fear, and they destroyed one another.

This is exactly what takes place on the day of the Lord Jesus Christ. He will return with His saints, who have received their priesthood. They will be full of the Spirit of God without measure and will be singing of the beauty of the Lord's holiness. When Christ, the high priest and captain of our faith, speaks the Word,

the nations will plunge into such confusion that they
will actually destroy themselves with their own weapons
(Zech. 14:13). Having embraced deception, those who
have worshiped the antichrist are now reaping its fruit,
confusion and death.

The prophet Zechariah wrote:

> And this shall be the plague wherewith the
> Lord will smite all the people that have fought
> against Jerusalem; Their flesh shall consume
> away while they stand upon their feet, and
> their eyes shall consume away in the their
> holes, and their tongue shall consume away
> in their mouth. . . And so shall be the plague
> of the horse, of the mule, of the camel, and
> of the ass, and of all the beasts that shall be
> in these tents, as this plague. (Zech. 14:12, 15)

In this passage, Zechariah gives us a prophetic account of the nations releasing their weapons upon one
another. From the description that he gives of the
plague, it appears that there will be a nuclear exchange.
They do to themselves what they intended to do to the
Lord and to His anointed: Hence, the fulfilling of the
law of sowing and reaping is evident.

As all of the nations plunge into chaos, the feet of
Christ will stand upon the mount of Olives, which is
before Jerusalem on the east. And the mount of Olives
shall cleave in the midst thereof toward the east and
toward the west, and there shall be a great valley: and
half of the mountain shall move toward the north and
half toward the south (see Zech. 14:4, 5). The surviv-

ing Jews will flee into this great valley. It is there that the Lord will protect them from this great holocaust as the kings of the earth destroy themselves with their own weapons.

The surviving Jews will behold the glory of the Lord. The veil will be removed from their eyes, and they will realize that they have been rejecting the Messiah, the Glory of Israel. There will then be mourning in Israel like never before. Here is where the Deliverer comes from Zion and banishes ungodliness from Jacob (Rom. 11:26). Christ will pour out a spirit of grace and supplication, so that when the nation of Israel looks upon Him whom they have pierced, they shall mourn for Him as one mourns for an only child. They will weep bitterly as one weeps over a firstborn (Zech. 12:10). The remnant of Israel will be reborn in a day (Isa. 66:8; Zech. 3:9).

As the end draws nigh, the thrones of the kingdom of darkness will be cast down and the heavens will be opened wide. And the Ancient of Days will come and give judgment in favor of the saints of the most high; the time has come for the saints to possess the kingdom (Dan. 7:22).

"The garment of the Ancient of Days will be white as snow, and the hair of His head like pure wool: His throne will be like the fiery flame, and His wheels as burning fire. A fiery stream will issue and come forth from before Him: a thousand thousands will minister unto Him, and ten thousand times ten thousand will stand before Him: the judgment will be set and the books will be opened" (Dan. 7:9, 10).

As He appears, the heavens will depart like a scroll

when it is rolled together. And every mountain and island will be moved out of their places. And the kings of the earth and the great men, the rich men, the chief captains and the mighty men will hide themselves in the dens and the rocks of the mountains. They will cry to the rocks of the mountains, "Fall on us, and hide us from the face of him that sitteth on the throne, and from the wrath of the Lamb: For the great day of his wrath is come; and who shall be able to stand?" Rev. 6:14–17; Isa. 2:10–22).

As the Ancient of Days appears above the earth, the blasphemous beast will be taken and slain and his body destroyed and given to the burning flame (Dan. 7:11).

Peace has been born! Like the head of a child emerging from the womb, through intense pain, the head of the seed that was sown in the womb of the earth has been revealed to be Jesus, the prince of peace. He will then deliver the kingdoms of the earth to God the Father; having put down all of the factious rulers and authorities and all powers of the universe (1 Cor. 15:24).

All of the peoples of the earth who have not been destroyed in this great conflict will then behold the Son of man (Jesus), coming with the clouds of heaven to the Ancient of Days (Dan. 7:13). This is an absolutely beautiful portrayal of the King of kings coming before the Father *with the bride at his side.*

Having already received our priestly inheritance of the unlimited infilling of the Spirit of God, the Church will now receive its rightful inheritance of the earth and the universe, over which it shall reign with Christ as kings. This event was forshadowed in the tabernacle in the wilderness. The tabernacle was completed with every detail in order, anointed with God's presence and went in to possess the promised inheritance, Canaan.

The bride of Christ (the Church) will receive title to the earth in the presence of all remaining flesh, as well as the heavenly host. Isaiah prophesied that every valley (the humble) shall be exalted, and every mountain and hill (the proud and arrogant) shall be made low. The crooked shall be made straight, and the rough places plain. And the glory of the Lord shall be revealed. *All flesh shall see it together*, for the mouth of the Lord has spoken it. (See Isa. 40:4, 5.)

As Christ victoriously comes before the Father in the presence of all creation, His glory shall be revealed. (This is, in part, His bride). There, He will receive dominion, glory and a kingdom so that all people, nations and languages should serve Him! His dominion shall be an everlasting dominion. It shall not pass away, and His kingdom shall not be destroyed (Dan. 7:14).

When the bride receives her glory with the Son of man, in clear view of all of God's creation above the earth, *all* of the creation (which has been held in captivity under sin's dominion), will rejoice. All creation eagerly awaits the revealing of the sons of God (Rom. 8:19).

Daniel says that the saints of the most high shall be given the kingdom, dominion and the greatness of the kingdom under the whole heaven (Dan. 7:27).

In a letter, John writes, "Behold, what manner of love the Father hath bestowed upon us, that we should be called the sons of God: therefore the world knoweth us not, because it knew him not. Beloved, now are we the sons of God, and it doth not yet appear what we shall be: but we know that, when he shall appear, we shall be like him; for we shall see him as he is. And every man that hath this hope in him purifieth himself, even as he is pure" (1 John 3:1-3).

Suggested Reading: Isa. 26:20, 21; Mal. 4:1-3; Isa. 34:1-8; Joel 2:1-11; Rev. 19:13; Joel 3:11-16; Isa. 63:1-6; Isa. 2:10-22.

10
Peace! Peace at Last!

With the coming of the Lord in power and glory, the great rebellion of the principalities of darkness (who have destroyed the earth), have been put down. Satan's dominion has been taken away, and he has been bound for a thousand years (Rev. 20:2).

The two seeds of truth and deception which have matured in the womb of the earth, and have brought forth fruit after their kind, have been harvested. The remnant of those nations which remain after this great conflict will be gathered to the valley of Jehoshaphat to be judged by Christ and His Church. They will be judged as nations, dependent upon how they have treated God's people.[1]

Upon the completion of these national judgments, Christ will establish His throne above all of the thrones of the earth and will reign for a thousand years (Rev. 20:4). Those who will be allowed to enter this millennium of peace will be the remnant of Israel, the bride of Christ, and a remnant of the gentiles. Although the remnant of the gentiles that have survived the tribulation did not receive Christ as their savior, they probably refused to submit to the antichrist. It is possible that they endeavored to harbor God's people during the tribulation period. Like Rahab the harlot, they will receive a portion of the blessing (Josh. 6:17, 25).

Like the mother who cuddles the newborn baby to her breast, the earth will now embrace a millennium of peace under the headship of Christ. It will be a thousand years before she passes the afterbirth of the sin nature of man.

The prophet Micah is one of the many prophets who give us foresight into the coming kindgom:

> But in the last days it shall come to pass, that the mountain of the house of the Lord shall be established in the top of the mountains, and it shall be exalted above the hills; and people shall flow unto it.
>
> And many nations shall come, and say, Come, and let us go up to the mountain of the Lord, and to the house of the God of Jacob; and he will teach us of his ways, and we will walk in his paths: for the law shall go forth of Zion, and the word of the Lord from Jerusalem.
>
> And he shall judge among many people, and rebuke strong nations afar off; and they shall beat their swords into plowshares, and their spears into pruninghooks: nation shall not lift up a sword against nation, neither shall they learn war any more.
>
> But they shall sit every man under his vine and under his fig tree; and none shall make

them afraid: for the mouth of the Lord of
hosts has spoken it. (Micah 4:1-4)

At the end of the thousand years, Satan will be
loosed. He will again stir the sin nature which remains
in the hearts of the men who were allowed to enter this
age of peace. He will go to the four quarters of the
earth and will deceive men, gathering together an army
of men whose number is as the sands of the sea.

This will be the final stages of labor, as the passing
of the placenta. Once more, men will seek to exalt
themselves above the Most High. They will compass
the camp of the saints about, and the beloved city
(Jerusalem). Then God will personally defend the saints
with fire from heaven, and will "devour" them (Rev.
20:7-15).

Then the devil will be taken and cast into the lake
of fire where the beast and the false prophet are. They
will be tormented by day and night, forever.

Then the second resurrection will come (Rev. 20:5).
This is the resurrection of the dead of all ages. It is
the great white throne judgment. Every man who has
ever lived—the dead of all ages, both small and great—
will stand before God, and the books of records will
be opened. Each man will be judged according to his
works. Every man whose name is not written in the
Lamb's book of life will be cast into the lake of fire
(Rev. 20:11-15).

The only people who will escape the great white
throne judgment are those who have received the mercy
of God through the blood of the Lamb—Jesus Christ.
These are those who judge themselves by the Word of

God prior to death (1 Cor. 11:31). They are lovers of God who have exercised their love through pursuit of Him and obedience to His Word. They are His Church, the ones who make up the first resurrection. Having previously judged themselves by the Word of God, they will not be subjected to the terrifying judgment of the great white throne. They are the bride of Christ, and will be at His side participating in the judgment of the world (1 Cor. 6:2).

With the completion of the great white throne judgment, death will be swallowed up in victory. The earth will pass away with a fervent heat, and God will create a new heaven and a new earth. He will then dwell with men, and will wipe away all tears from their eyes. And there shall be no more death, sorrow, or crying. Neither shall there be any more pain, for the former things shall pass away.

He that sits upon the throne will say, "Behold, I make all things new. . . I will give unto him that is athirst of the fountain of the water of life freely. He that overcometh shall inherit all things; and I will be his God, and he shall be my son. But the fearful, and unbelieving, and the abominable, and murderers, and whoremongers, and sorcerers, and idolaters, and all liars, shall have their part in the lake which burneth with fire and brimstone: which is the second death. . .

And, behold, I come quickly; and my reward is with me, to give every man according as his work shall be.

I am Alpha and Omega, the beginning and the end, the first and the last. Blessed are they that do his commandments, that they may have right to the tree of life. . . And the Spirit and the bride say, Come. And let him that heareth say, Come. And let him that is athirst come. And whosoever will, let him take the water of life freely. (Rev. 21:5, 6–8; 22:12–14, 17).

If you do not desire to love the Lord your God with all of your heart, or to have your mind renewed by His Word, or to have the inner motivations of your heart conformed to His image, then your name is not written in the Lamb's book of life. For the test of salvation is not in the things that you know, or in the works that you do or in the things that you say; rather, it is in the renewing of your heart and mind, by His engrafted word. If you desire Him, pursue Him: He will form His nature within you.

11
The Serpent's Third Greatest Deception

The doctrine that Jesus would not allow His beloved to experience the great tribulation has permeated contemporary theology. It appeals to our flesh to believe that God would rapture us away from any intense stress or discomfort. But the harvest of the Church (wheat) will not be done prematurely; it will continue to grow into maturity alongside the tare. Both the wheat and the tare will be harvested together to stand in their alloted place at the end of this present age. Once the wheat is harvested, there will be no reason to allow the earth to continue in its present state.

The church should do four things:

(1) Know the signs that God has given, to identify the man of sin when he is revealed;

(2) Anticipate a great falling away of many professing Christians;

(3) Prepare mentally and spiritually for a time of tribulation such as the world has never known;

(4) Seek to understand God's purpose in the great tribulation, as it concerns all of His creation, no longer focusing on personal desires.

People shudder when they consider the prospect of having to endure the chaos of the closing scenes of this present age. They do not understand that *the battle which rages inside of each and every one of us is the greatest conflict known to man. Having gained victory over the inner man through Christ, nothing else can defeat us!* If we press on to discover the victory over ourselves that comes through a living relationship with Christ, and the peace that reigns in our hearts from devotion to Him, there is nothing—nothing at all— that can defeat or discourage us, *not even death.*

Has refusal to believe that we will experience the great tribulation caused the Church to be slumbering in the day? Are the itching ears of Christ's bride being scratched? Christians are taught that they will be instantly removed with no warning: But the Church should be exhorted to watch, to keep its lamps trim, and to know the times and seasons. God's Word has opened the future, not for the appeasing of curiosity, but to prepare, exhort, and sober His people so that they might stand in the coming days of calamity.

Many professing Christians, however, are living according to the prophetic insight of Jesus concerning the Laodicean church.

Today's church is rich with the knowledge of God's Word more than any of the saints of the ages past. Yet selfishness, irresponsibility and apathy are rampant. Like butterflies, many flit from fellowship to fellowship, gleaning the nectar of knowledge yet giving nothing to the flower. Puffed with knowledge, many have carelessly spawned a critical spirit toward one another, thereby causing many to be despondent, losing touch with the love of God which first sparked their hope of salvation.

Where is the broken and contrite heart that Christians should seek? (See Ps. 51:7.)

Christians should be like Enoch. Enoch *walked* with God. He sought the person of God. He laid aside every weight and sin that would prevent his fellowship with God. In faith, Enoch sought to be obedient to God.

Jesus is the Word of God made flesh (the torn Veil between God and man, according to Heb. 10:19–20) through Him we have access into the very presence of the Father. The New Testament calls Him Savior twenty-four times, and Lord seven hundred and three times. Do we kneel to Him or expound Him?

In all of our "learning" of Him, have we closed our ears to His voice? He is moving among the Church, earnestly seeking those who will open the doors of true repentance and sup with Him at the table of His Lordship. We should, therefore, eat the bread of truth and drink the cup of covenant, purposing in our hearts to resist sin even unto the shedding of blood.

There is coming a falling away! *Doctrine cannot sustain a man!* Those who do not abide in Him will be stripped away. Seek Him while He can be found. The spring of the ages has come, and the fig tree (Israel) has put forth its leaves. The summer heat is nigh, and the vine will cast its untimely fruit. Those who endure will become fully formed, drinking in the latter rains of God's Spirit before the harvest. Those who are rooted in Him will bring forth a mature fruit of holiness. Their fruit will be delightful to the eye and pleasant to the King.

The vine will be pruned to the stump, and only those who have the Word of God rooted deep in their hearts, without exposure to the heat of the summer sun, will remain to ripen to maturity.

We Christians must open our eyes, observe the times, and discover the Christ who brings peace in the inner man. Let us trim the carbon of self-centeredness from our lamps and keep them filled to the brim with the oil of His Spirit. The vineyard shall come to maturity and the beauty of the husbandman will be seen in the midst. The glory of the Lord shall be revealed when the Church, adorned in all-consuming love for the Father, stands in maturity in the earth and reflects the light and glory of the Spirit of God.

The doctrine that Jesus would not allow His beloved to experience the great tribulation has permeated contemporary Christian doctrine. It appeals to us to believe that God will deliver us from any discomfort and rapture us into ecstasy. The fruit of this doctrine has caused many within the Church to be lax, passive in their pursuit of God, and unconcerned about present world conditions. Therefore, we are terrifyingly unprepared for the greatest onslaught of unrestrained sin the world has ever known. This doctrine is *the serpent's third greatest deception!*[1]

Suggested readings: Rev. 2:7, 11, 17, 26; 3:5, 12, 21; Matt. 24:13; Col. 1:27.

Footnotes

Chapter 1

[1]Ham fathered Canaan, Babylon, Egypt, Philistim (the Philistines), Sodom, Gomorrah, and a host of other nations which inhabit Africa. They all have a history of heavy involvement in immorality and the occult. These nations have fathered multitudes of idolatrous religions, incorporating the most grotesque sins, and have been an abomination to Jehovah (the Lord God). The Scriptures speak of them with negative connotations, and infer their eventual demise.

To state that all of the descendants of Ham are wicked would be as incorrect as stating that all of the descendants of Shem are righteous. However, the immoral character of Ham was recognized by his father Noah, and that immoral character occasioned the curse that follows the descendants of Ham to this day (See Gen. 9:25).

The Lord has used the descendants of Ham to teach the nature of the tare, as He has used the descendants of Shem (Israel), to teach the nature of the wheat.

Chapter 2

[1]God told Israel through Moses that they were to sow their land and gather the fruits thereof in six-year

periods. The seventh years were to be sabbaths of rest unto the land, letting it rest and lie still (Exod. 23:10, 11; Lev. 25:4). It was also to be a time of releasing debts to neighbors and brethren (Deut. 15:1, 2).

For 490 years, Israel never observed any of the sabbatical years. Therefore, Jehovah collected His sabbatical years all at once. He took Israel into Babylon for seventy years of captivity, and gave the land its rest. [490 years, divided by 7 = 70 years.] (See 2 Chron. 36:21).

²There is a verse of Scripture which is regularly used to prove that no man knows the day or the hour of the Day of the Lord, or our gathering together unto Him. This verse is: "But of that day and hour knoweth no man, no, not the angels of heaven, but my Father only." (Matt. 24:36).

To date, this statement is correct. No man presently knows the day or hour. However, careful observation of this passage shows us that it is spoken in the *present tense*.

Jesus gave us points of reference concerning His second coming and the gathering of the bride, as He did concerning His first coming. These are reference points that are yet future to us, as the decree to rebuild Jerusalem was yet future to Daniel. These points are given so that the last generation of the true bride will not be caught by surprise, as were the Jews on the day that Jesus rode into Jerusalem.

He warns us to watch (Matt. 24:42; 25:13; Luke 12:37; 21:36). So do Paul and Peter (1 Thess. 5:6; 1 Peter 4:7). Do not be caught as though a thief had entered your house! We are not to be in darkness that

that day should overtake us as a thief (1 Thess. 5:4).

The intent of this work is to clearly reveal a definite chain of events which will transpire prior to the gathering of the bride and His coming in power and glory. These events give us the times and seasons, so that the last generation of the church will not be caught unaware. Jesus gave us all of these insights so that we would know when His coming was near, even at the door (Matt. 24:33). There is no question that Noah and Lot knew exactly what time it was. Only those doomed for judgment could not discern the times.

Chapter 3

¹If the bride was removed prior to the revealing of the man of sin, then the passage in 2 Thess. 2:1–4 would need to be taken out of the book. Not to mention the theological gymnastics we would have to perform to deal with the following four Scriptures:

(1) Dan. 7:21—"I beheld, and the same horn [the antichrist] made war with the saints, and prevailed against them."

(2) Dan. 7:25—"And he [the antichrist] shall speak great words against the most High, and shall wear out the saints of the most High, and think to change times and laws: and they [the saints] shall be given into his hand until a time and times and the dividing of time" (that is, for three-and-one-half years).

(3) Rev. 12:17—"And the dragon [the antichrist] was wroth with the woman [Israel], and went to make war with the remnant of her seed, which keep the commandments of God, and have the testimony of Jesus Christ [the saints].

(4) Rev. 13:7—"And it was given unto him [the anti-christ] to make war with the saints, and to overcome them: and power was given him over all kindreds, and tongues, and nations."

The church will go through the time of great tribulation that will climax this present age. It will not be a negative experience but, rather, a positive. Those who trust in God will see His Word being fulfilled. They will lift their heads, knowing His redemption draws nigh.

Chapter 4
¹The book of Daniel is a tremendous gift of prophecy to us. It has been given so that, as history unfolds, God's people would see His divine control of world events and not lose hope. Daniel was shown the rise and fall of all of the world's great kingdoms, as well as the first and second coming of Christ. He was shown that the Babylonian kingdom he resided in would be overthrown by the Medo-Persian kingdom; that the Medo-Persian kingdom would be overthrown by the Greek kingdom; and that the Greek kingdom would be overthrown by the Roman kingdom. However, the Roman kingdom was never to be overthrown militarily, but would continue until the latter days, when out of the remnant of this deteriorated kingdom there would rise up a ten-nation confederacy.

History fulfilled Daniel's visions, just as God had said it would, for each kingdom has come and gone. But we have never lost the effects of the Roman kingdom entirely. Its religion and government have continued to influence the world throughout modern times. And despite intense efforts on the part of many men, no man has succeeded in reuniting the Roman empire.

Now the scene is changing. Out of the remains of the Roman empire, a ten-nation confederacy has emerged—uniting the heart of the old kingdom. This confederacy (the European Economic Community or the Common Market) is probably the one foretold by the prophet Daniel. Coincidence? By no means. God's Word is being fulfilled, and the world's stage is being set for its final and greatest conflict.

One of Daniel's visions of this fourth kingdom is recorded as follows: "After this I saw in the night visions, and behold a fourth beast, dreadful and terrible, and strong exceedingly; and it had great iron teeth: it devoured and brake in pieces, and stamped the residue with the feet of it: and it was diverse from all the beasts that were before it; and it had ten horns. I considered the horns, and, behold, there came up among them another little horn, before whom there were three of the first horns plucked up by the roots: and, behold, in this horn were eyes like the eyes of man, and a mouth speaking great things" (Dan. 7:7, 8).

These two verses speak of the rise of the ten horns out of the fourth beast (the Roman empire), and of a little horn which will rise up among the ten. We are told that these horns represent kings. "And the ten horns out of this kingdom are ten kings that shall arise: and another shall rise after them; and he shall be diverse from the first, and he shall subdue three kings" (Dan. 7:24).

The topic of this chapter is the king (the little horn) who arises from among the ten kings (horns) and sub- dues three of them. He is the one that the Church should anticipate. He is the key figure in discerning the times. May the Spirit of God give Christians wisdom and discernment to rightly divide His Word.

Chapter 6

[1]Let us identify the court which is without the temple (Rev. 11:2). In the days of the Old Testament, when Israel was God's prominent testimony in the earth, the outer court was also called the court of Gentiles. It could be frequented by Gentiles and unclean persons. Only Israel was allowed to enter into the inner temple, to make sin offerings at the altar, and to worship therein.

Now things are reversed. We are in the time of the Gentiles, or the church age. Israel is blinded (Rom. 11:25); they cannot see beyond the veil, which is Christ (Heb. 10:20). The nation, as a whole, has rejected the Messiah. They are not able to enter through the veil (which is Jesus) into the presence of God in the holy of holies. They are, therefore, spiritually placed in the outer court of the unclean, unable to enter into the heavenly holy of holies.

Their refusal to accept the cleansing work of the blood of the Lord Jesus Christ has caused them to remain outside of the throne room where the atoning blood was sprinkled, wherein the mercy seat of God resided, overshadowing the tablets of the covenant of the law. They will remain in the outer court until the fulfilling of Zech. 12:10, whereupon at the physical return of Jesus, the eyes of Israel will be opened.

Jesus is the veil that prevents Israel from beholding the glory of God. Because of Israel's hardness of heart, that veil will remain untorn for them as a nation until they behold the scars in the hands and feet of the Messiah on the mount of Olives.

Through the church age, until the second coming of the Lord, only the bride of Christ (the Church) is able to see through the torn veil of the body of Jesus into the holy of holies. That is where the glory of God, and the cleansing power of the pure blood of sprinkling, rest upon the mercy seat which is above, and is superior to, the tablets of the covenent of law.

Jesus is the veil between God and man—between the spiritual and the physical world. He is also the absolute fullness of the Word of God. In other words, there is— between the physical world of man and the spiritual world of the living God—an impassable gulf or barrier that cannot be crossed by the natural man unless he uses the only door. That door is the Word of God, Jesus is the Word of God made flesh (John 1:14).

The rending of that veil (the crucifixion) has allowed the light of God to penetrate into our world, thereby giving us clear perception into the heart of God. His light is the fullness of His Word, manifested in the flesh and illumined by His spirit. The veil, which has prevented our vision of God, has been torn from top to bottom, making it possible for us to behold the glory of the Father through the completed work of the cross.

As Jesus brings the Temple of God (the Church) into completion in the earth, and we come to the unity of the faith and the knowledge of the Son of God, we will become a perfect man unto the measure of the stature of the fullness of Christ (Eph. 3:14). We will corporately behold the Word of God in His entirety, penetrating the veil of God's Word with our spiritual eyes and beholding the glory of the Father of our Redeemer. Our eyes will be steadfast upon Him and our desire will be to be like Him.

In that day, the church will walk with God, as did Enoch. Then He will take us, the mature harvest of the seed of God's Word. We will then be united with the saints of all ages, and Jesus will present us to the Father. We will be a Holy Tabernacle of men made righteous, fitly framed together by the Master Architect for the Spirit of God to dwell in without measure.

Summarizing the content of the first three verses of Rev. 11, we see these four things:

(1) The church (Temple) has grown into maturity and is measured for the final harvest;

(2) Israel is still rejecting Jesus as the Messiah. As a nation, they dwell spiritually in the outer court of the heavenly temple (the court for the unclean). They have not been cleansed by the blood of Jesus Christ;

(3) Sin has grown into maturity. The antichrist has revealed himself in the holy place, desecrating it and trampling the holy city with his armies;

(4) As the final three-and-one-half year countdown of this age is begun, God will raise two witnesses to represent and encourage the Church. The Church's faith is being severely tested, in order that patience might have its perfect work and that we may be perfect and entire, lacking nothing of the character of God (James 1:4).

Chapter 8

[1]The church will be adorned (or rewarded), for her works: (Rev. 19:8; 2 Cor. 5:10; 1 Cor. 3:11–15; Matt. 25:14–30; Luke 19:11–27).

Chapter 9

[1]Daniel 7:25 states that the saints shall be given into the hand of the antichrist for "a time and times and the dividing of time." Bible scholars generally agree that this is a time frame of three-and-one-half years.

Since lunar years were used by the Jews, and are regularly accepted in the interpretation of biblical prophecies, the application of the lunar year in this passage would seem most appropriate.

A lunar year is 360 days long. If one were to multiply 360 days by 3½, the result would be 1,260 days.

There are five separate events that occur during the 1,290 day reign of the antichrist. Each of them is 1,260 days. These are:

(1) The saints are given into the hand of the antichrist for 3½ years (1,260 days)—(Dan. 7:25);

(2) The gentile armies tread Jerusalem for 1,260 days (42 lunar months = 1,260 days)—(Rev. 11:2);

(3) The two witnesses shall prophesy, smiting the earth with plagues for 1,260 days (Rev. 11:3);

(4) The Jews shall flee to the wilderness for 1,260 days (Rev. 12:6);

(5) The antichrist is empowered 1,260 days (42 lunar months) to blaspheme God, make war with the saints overcoming them, rule the earth and demand that the whole earth worship him (Rev. 13:5–8).

Daniel 12:11 states the antichrist will be alloted 1,290 days. His reign will be overthrown by the coming of the Lord (Dan. 8:25; Rev. 19:19). This 1290 day time period is thirty days beyond this allotted 1260 day dominion over the saints, Jerusalem and the rest of the world (1,290 − 1,260 = 30).

This period of thirty days (or less) is allotted for two events: The marriage of the Lamb to his espoused bride in the heavens; and the outpouring of the wrath of God in the earth.

The man of sin will have dominion until the Church is removed. From that point on, the earth will be in utter chaos as the seven angels pour out the wrath of God. In a desperate attempt to maintain his throne, the antichrist will deceive the kings of the earth and cause them to gather at the Valley of Megiddo (Armageddon) to resist the coming of the Lord (Rev. 19:19; Ps. 2).

Chapter 10
[1]National judgments in the valley of Jehoshaphat (see Joel 3:1-2, Matt. 25:31-46; I Cor. 6:2).

From the day of the Lord's coming (which transpires 1,290 days after the revealing of the man of sin in the Holy Place), until the completion of these national judgments, there will be forty-five days. Daniel recorded that those who come to the 1,335th day are blessed [1,290 + 45 = 1,335]—(Dan. 12:12).

Chapter 11
[1]To state that the rapture doctrine, as is commonly taught, is the serpent's third greatest deception con-

sistently arouses the question, "What are the first two?"

There is little doubt that the first, and greatest, deception Satan ever wrought on man is that he could be independent of and equal to the most high God. From the fall of Adam to the present time, the natural man refuses to honor and love the God of creation.

The second greatest deception that Satan has wrought on man is like the first. Men have vainly imagined that they could approach God on the basis of their own good works. However, the righteousness of man is as filthy rags in the light of the righteousness of God (Isa. 64:6).